Unmasked To Heal

Kim Johnson
Roberta Phillips
Cynthia Rose
Crystal Rivera
Simene' Walden

Unmasked to Heal by SIMENE' WALDEN

Published by THE STUDENT TEACHER

P.O. BOX 813, SAVAGE, MD 20763

www.simenwalden.com

© 2019 Simene' Walden

ISBN:978-0-9997987-9-9

To book any other authors, please contact them directly.

If you are interested in discounts for bulk purchases or to use any part of this book, please email: simene@simenewalden.com

Cover design by SPG Design | Editing and formatting by Tru Inc.

All scripture quotations, unless otherwise noted, are taken from the King James Bible and New Living Translation. All rights reserved.

Scripture quotations, noted *NKJV*, are taken from the New King James Bible. Copyright ©1979, 1980, 1982, 1984 by Thomas Nelson, Inc. Used by permission. All rights reserved.

First Printing August 2019

Printed in the United States of America

Why Unmasked to Heal?

The first Unmasked event evolved from a small group meeting and has grown to a sought-after movement within a few months. It began as eleven courageous men and women, from all walks of life, gathered together to share their personal stories of healing, deliverance, and breakthrough. Their testimonies have been some of the realest and most relevant stories I have ever heard.

The Unmasked movement has now emerged the Unmasked to Heal anthology. In this book, five courageous women have also dared to share their intimate stories publicly. It is a great read for someone who has experienced childhood trauma or who may wrestle with addictions in the form of drugs or sex. For the person who feels rejected or oppressed after divorce or crisis situations, this book is a must have. If you have ever sought to discover your true identity or self-worth, you need this book!

You will be encouraged after each chapter in Unmasked to Heal. The authors are living proof that there is redemption, forgiveness, and hope at the end of a seemingly hopeless situation. You will be inspired to keep striving and to press forward in the midst of your trials.

Discover how you can uncover God's healing power and allow Him to remove the masks that hide you behind the pain of your past. As a result, you too will be able to get past the shame, guilt, and frustration that prevents you from moving forward. Let Unmasked to Healed show you the way to walk in your newness of life.

A Note from The Visionary

As the lead author behind this anthology, at first, I had the hardest time penning my chapter. I asked, "Why Lord?"

He revealed to me that my motive was not pure when I originally thought of the idea for this project. I had been more concerned about the monetary benefits instead of consulting with God for His guidance. So, I repented.

I realized, God had chosen me as a catalyst in His healing process, and money is the last thing I should have been focusing on. For years, the women featured in this book had refused to share the details of their personal experiences. Now, after receiving God's forgiveness and focusing on His plan for Unmasked to Heal, I know that my obedience will bring profit to the Kingdom of God which is my desire.

Simene' Walden

Acknowledgments

Words cannot express my gratitude and appreciation to God for the ability to carry a project of this magnitude from conception to completion.

I personally thank each of you women, Mrs. Roberta Phillips, Ms. Crystal Rivera, Ms. Cynthia Rose, and Ms. Kim Johnson for trusting me with your stories. After reading them, it took weeks upon weeks for me to process them all. God is amazing! He has worked wonders in each of your lives. I am honored that you chose to work with me on this project.

To every mentor, accountability partner, and friend, thank you. Thank you for speaking life into me when I wanted to give up and die. To every person who has supported the vision of The Student Teacher, thank you.

To you, who are reading this right now, thank you. May God exceed your expectations with this book. May your healing process begin or be expedited, in Jesus' Name.

To my parents, Thurman & Linda, thank you for making me. I hope I am making you proud. Mom you have been there for me since I was sperm in your womb until now. I can never thank you enough for sticking with me through all of my trials. I love you both.

Simene' Walden

Thank You Jesus, for my Mom and Grandma (deceased), who were adamant that my foundation was immersed in the Word of God. Without His Word, I could not and would not be standing today.

Thank you, to my family and friends who have encouraged me and endured my strong will and personality.

Thank you, to Pastor Nike Wilheims of Temple of Praise International Church in Beltsville, Maryland, for the delivery of the Word on my first visit. The Word of God continues to propel and motivate me to walk in my purpose.

Thank you, to Simene' Walden, The Student Teacher, and Publisher, for the opportunity to "unmask" on paper. Telling my story is what I have desired to do for many years. You are AWE inspiring!

Cynthia Rose

Thank you, God, for saving ME from me!

To Mom and Dad, Ethyl B. and Henry T. Hayes. There would be no me without them. Before they ever thought of me, GOD had brought them together. I thank them for their second baby girl, ME!

To my sister Brigette, thank you for loving me through life. You have always been there for me at my lowest moments. I thank God for you!

To Donald, the *"LOVE" of my life and my biggest supporter;* You are the man who loves me unconditionally and accepts me for who I am.

Donald, you are God sent. God heard my request and you are everything I asked for. I thank God for you fulfilling my dream. You are the nicest man I know! I LOVE you more and more each day!

When I was gracefully broken, there was a crack in my life that felt like death; yet every time I fell, I landed gently with the help of angels. But God! God met me in my pain!

Crystal Hayes Rivera

Table of Contents

The Fear Factor

Healing from "The Fear Factor" by Roberta Phillips

The Beginning of Fear
"Train up a child…" (Proverbs 22:6)

I can recall sitting at the kitchen table with two of my elder siblings while doing homework. After I became stuck on a math problem, I called out to my siblings for help, but to no avail. So, I climbed underneath the kitchen table and grabbed a hold of my sister's leg and began shaking it.

At the time, my grandparents cared for us each day after school, while our mom was at work. Both my grandparents were brought up with a strict, *"train up a child…" mentality (Proverbs 22:6).*

This particular evening, grandma was in the front room of the house watching television. She could always be found there, after all of the household chores were completed. My grandpa wasn't too far away; five feet on his left side were my siblings and I, and another five feet our grandmother was on the right side of him. Together, they usually kept us in close proximity to them to ensure that we didn't misbehave.

Grandpa sat against the wall wearing blue overalls while he fiddled with something in his hands. Suddenly, he was alerted by the sounds of my little voice coming from beneath the dining room table. I cannot imagine what he may have been thinking at the time; however, by his reaction, it was nothing good. I wonder if memories of his history replayed in his mind to make him react in such a way.

In an instant, Grandpa had snatched me so fast from under the table. I never saw him coming, and I didn't have time to run. All of a sudden, I was looking at the ceiling with my feet in his hands while being held up from the floor.

The spanking felt as if he were using a thick leather belt, but it was actually his very strong hands. I will never, ever forget that day. Even now, if I think long enough, I can still feel the sting of that whipping as if it happened yesterday. What lessons did I learn? Ask someone else for help with my homework, preferably an adult, and it was safer to ask Grandpa since he was the disciplinarian of the house.

As for my mother, she was an entirely different story. If I was ever disobedient, she would spank me even after I had been spanked by my grandfather. They were from what we called, "old school," which meant that if one adult spanked you, they passed on the information to your parents, and you were sure to get spanked a second time.

My mother had a method to her madness; she would make us either lie across the bed or stand and touch our toes while she spanked us. I know somebody reading this knows exactly what I am talking about. Have you ever had feelings of fear, yet, felt loved all at the same time?

My mother's spankings almost always came with a note attached that said, *"It's going to hurt me more than it hurts you."* For the record, I never believed that statement since I was the one in pain.

Once I became a parent, my perspective changed. I finally understood that the pain my mother spoke about in her note wasn't a physical pain, but an emotional one. She was speaking from her heart. She did not enjoy giving spankings, but it was necessary to keep us from repeating the action.

It is the same way with our Heavenly Father. He loves us so much that He also chastens and corrects us. Oftentimes, we return back to the same sin only to be corrected again. God will first correct us in small, subtle ways, and then take drastic measures when we continue in disobedience. Even so, my mother's love could not prepare me for the mental, physical and emotional pain that awaited me in the future.

Hello Fear
"God has not given us…" (2 Timothy 1:7)

When I was seven years old, my mother decided to move our family to another state in hopes of providing a better life for us. A friend of my mothers who lived in Kansas City, Missouri allowed us to stay with her until my mother was able to get back on her feet.

The friend also hosted other families in her home. When we arrived, I remember being immediately separated from our mother. Note: It is important to pay attention to all "red flags" from others, but especially when there are small children involved.

My mother agreed to stay in the garage which had been converted into a two-bedroom home just outside of the main house. My siblings and I were moved to the main house along with other children and their parents. My mother's decision to live separately from us would change the course of my life for the next eighteen years.

The following morning, I woke up completely soaked in my own urine. My mother had gone to work, and I was left to fend for myself in my new surroundings. I did not know anyone and had to rely on others to take care of me.

3

I confided in an older girl who stayed in the room with me. She ran to get one of the adults who then sent me to the dining area. As I entered the doorway of the room, I saw the owner of the house seated in a chair. She had an audience of the other children who were seated on the floor in front of her.

She told me to bring to her the piece of carpet that I had urinated on. She directed me to place it on the floor between her legs. She then ordered me to kneel down and put my face in the wet spot, like a dog, as everyone stood around watching. I heard chuckles from some of the kids, but not one single person uttered a word in my defense; not even my siblings.

After being completely humiliated, I was sent back to the bedroom that I shared with my sister and two other girls. I was made to stand with my back against the wall with both of my arms extended and the palm of my hands facing upward. I was given a large and heavy book to hold on my tired arms for what seemed like an eternity. This was only the beginning of the abuse I would endure while living in this strange home.

Each day, the abuse was escalated by either the owner or the young adult males who lived there. Often, I was severely disciplined for behaving as a "normal" seven-year-old child would. It was later revealed that my female abuser suffered from her own brokenness and carried anger towards her mother, which was now being directed at me. I also believe that her constant abuse of me prompted the young men living there to make daily attempts of having sexual contact with me.

One of the young men manipulated me into going with him upstairs to another boy's room to see the fish in the fish tank. Once there, he exposed himself to me and began to fondle his genitals. I bolted downstairs to the bedroom that I shared with the other three girls. I was traumatized. I remember hiding on the floor with the cover pulled over my head as my body continued to shake in fear.

The eldest girl, who was 16 years old, entered the room to find me still shaking on the floor. She helped me up and told me not to be afraid. She said I would be safe lying in bed with her. I believed her and climbed into her bed.

She lay behind me and began to rub her body against mine in sexual manner while her hands explored my private body parts. At first, I froze. Then, as if by a sudden impulse, I leaped from her bed and landed back to the floor which became my place of safety.

I was still on the floor and back under the covers when I felt a tug on the covers followed by a familiar voice...it was my sister. From that point, whenever I was in danger, God would miraculously direct her to come and save me.

Acting Out Fear
"Do not provoke…" Ephesians 6:4

The days that followed were full of terrifying events. I did not know what I would experience when I went to bed at night or when I woke up in the morning. Each passing day was a living nightmare. I quickly learned to internalize my feelings and avoided expressing myself to anyone.

I did not share with anyone what was happening to me, especially not my mom. As a child, I thought my mother was either too busy or she simply would not believe me if I told her what was going on. Besides that, I was told not to open my mouth; so, I continued to suffer in silence.

Growing up, my siblings and I were taught two very important lessons; never talk back to an adult, and whatever an adult says is the truth. As a result, I always thought I was being obedient when I kept my feelings of hurt and anger bottled up on the inside. It had become my way of life.

Thankfully, it had been revealed to my mom about the abuse going on in the house. Shortly thereafter, we moved out. By this time, my mental state and physical body had been damaged, but not totally irreparable.

Once we moved, there was a shift in my mother's behavior; she was no longer the same person. I can only imagine it was the guilt she must have felt after discovering what had been going on inside the home. We never discussed any of the horrible events, and she told my siblings and I that we must never tell our other family what happened, but especially not our grandparents.

Over time, my mother began to put distance between herself and her children. She was rarely available to care for us or to show us love as she once had done. Confused, I rebelled and became angry at her. I started "acting out" which led to her become excessive in her disciplinary tactics.

Her response to my behavior only intensified my anger towards my her. I progressed from looking up to my mom to being disconnected from her and disrespectful to her. I felt like she didn't care, so neither did I. As I grew older, my actions would continue to demonstrate that same "I don't care" attitude.

During my teenage years, I turned to the streets for solace. I began smoking weed, drinking and soon became sexually promiscuous. My brother looked after my sister and I whenever he wasn't out in the streets; however, most of the time, my sister and I looked after each other.

I can't describe the level of hate and anger I carried on the inside of me; I was a ticking time bomb, waiting to explode. At times, I would get into fights. I would fight if I thought someone looked at me the wrong way or said the wrong thing to me. I would fight so hard, that I would black out. Only the sight of blood or the voice of my mother or sister could bring me out of my trance.

There were times when my own brother would wake me from my sleep to fight with me. My brother and I fought so much, that my mother put him out of our home. I blamed myself when he left even when I knew it wasn't my fault. At the age of thirteen, I lived in constant fear and blamed myself for the mistakes that were caused by others. It was a very dark season in my life.

Releasing Fear
"Don't be anxious..." Philippians 4:6-7

I accepted Jesus Christ as my Lord and Savior at the age of 25, and on my 25th birthday. It was a year and a half after my second eldest daughter and my aunt had passed away. It was also eleven months to the day, that the father of my three eldest children died and nine months after the death of my cousin. The four deaths, along with the deaths of a host of close friends in between, caused me to become numb to life. I changed for the worst and began mingling with the wrong crowd of people and started doing the things I never imagined I would do.

Little did I know; God had a plan that was greater than the plan I had intended for my life. Looking back, I know that He had to sit me down to stop me from running wild.

In November of 1994, I was incarcerated. I was angry at God for not allowing me to live life on my own terms. A month later, I had had enough of doing things my own way. I completely surrendered to God's way and allowed Him to love me back to life.

That one day in December, I entered into my jail cell and He was there waiting to receive me with open arms. I cried out to the Lord and pleaded to him to rescue me from myself. Since that day, my life has never been the same.

My journey has not been easy; yet, I wouldn't trade it for nothing. In the book of *Isaiah 61:1-3*, God promised to give me *"beauty for ashes, the oil of joy instead of mourning and a garment of praise instead of a spirit of despair."* He has done that and more.

Over the last 25+ years, I have learned that no one can tell you neither how to heal, when your healing is over, nor what parts you should or shouldn't be healed from. This story is my truth, and I have gained healing by releasing it so others can also be healed. As I have entered into the year of 2019, I also ushered in my release and unmasked that which I had covered and internalized for forty-two long years.

Unmasked Fear
I've learned to be content…Philippians 4:11-13

I am now learning to confess my sins daily and to walk fearlessly by reminding myself that *"God has not giving me the spirit of fear, but of love and a sound mind,"* (2 Timothy 1:7).

I have been together with my husband for twenty-two years, and we have been married for nineteen of them. God has blessed our union with four amazing and gifted children and one grand-diamond.

I currently co-own a delivery business with my husband. I am also in the process of launching my own ministry, "Mirror Image," which is a non-profit organization that caters to broken women of all ages.

I serve has as an Evangelist Missionary and Prayer Warrior at Trinity Temple Church of God in Christ (C.O.G.I.C.), in Grandview, Missouri, where I have been a member for the past eight years.

My hope is that after reading my story you can see your own way out of an abusive situation. You may need to change your environment or the company of familiar faces that you are accustomed to being around. Beware, instead of providing strength to you, they may be crippling you.

Dare to live your greatest life; the God purposed life. Living a purposed life is not always easy, but your hill and valley experiences will be worth it in the end.

In the resource section of this book, I have recommended a few titles that have helped and empowered me along my journey to unmasking fear. It is my hope that you allow them to minister healing to you.

In closing, never give up on yourself because God will never leave you. Be encouraged, even when it seems as though God is silent. Trust that he is working on your behalf and, *"all things are working together for your good"* *(Romans 8:28)*. Remember, I am praying for you…May God bless you!

Roberta Phillips has always had a heart to serve those who are less fortunate than herself. She has worked as a nursing assistant for the past 27 years. She will attend Pen Valley Community College in the spring of 2019, where she will study for her degree in nursing, alongside her second eldest daughter.

Roberta is a catalyst for broken women with the belief that God can fix anything. Her mission in life is to make sure that when in her presence, every broken woman is left feeling different than when she came.

She lives in Belton, Missouri with her husband, four children and grandchild.

Connect with Roberta Phillips - Adidaj@yahoo.com.

The Untold Story

Healing from "The Untold Story" by Kim Johnson
Pittsburg, Pennsylvania: Where it all began.

For the most part, my earliest memories growing up had been good. However, most of my memories have been shadowed with the knowledge that my parents were unhappy while seeming to be happy. Our family did a lot of fun things, so no one on the outside would ever even think that anything was wrong.

I am the middle child of a total of three children. My brother is twenty months older than I, and I am nineteen months older than my sister. Honestly, I have no memory of ever "liking" my siblings. I loved them, we played together, but I did not like them. I wish my feelings for them had been different, but they didn't change, at least not until later in life.

I was in second grade when I sexually abused by five fifth graders who decided it was ok for them to have their way with me. Not too long after that, my family soon moved to different subdivision in the city of Pittsburgh. I was happy to attend a new school, but the kids at the new school were not so welcoming. The rest of my second-grade year through the fifth grade, I became a victim of bullying. I was a good child who didn't get in trouble, and because of that, I was called "Ms. Goodie Two-Shoes." When the kids saw that these words did not offend me, they began to hit on me. I was threatened almost every day by someone saying they were going to beat me up after school. The threats continued throughout my elementary years.

From the age of seven up until I was fifteen, I was molested in my home right under my parents' nose. I assume that they didn't know about it. If by chance they had known, no one said anything about it. It was during these years in my childhood that several family members began to have their own way with me. The abuse happened so often; it became normal for me. One of my abusers knew that once I began menstruating, I could become pregnant so he stopped. I wish other family members had felt the same, but unfortunately, the abuse continued. At a young age, I made a vow to myself that I didn't need anyone to love me; I would love myself. I equated sex to love, and at age eight, masturbation became a thing for me.

Pornography was also introduced to me at an early age. It started at nine years old when I was flipping through various magazines. I was thirteen when my youth choir director showed a pornographic video to me and one of my friends. We ran out of her house, but we never said a word to anyone. Years later, those images that I had seen would come back to haunt me.

By the age of eleven, I hated my life with a passion and began having suicidal thoughts. After several failed suicide attempts, I was so angry at God because He didn't just let me die! Emotionally, I was in a dark and lonely place.

It was in high school when I realized that I was intrigued by the female anatomy. I felt super weird about how it made me feel. I struggled the most when I went to the gym. I would even rush to change my clothes, so I could get to gym class. It was also in high school that my friends started calling me names like gay, fag and Tomboy.

My demeanor shifted. I carried a "you can't hurt me anymore" toughness with my hands clutched in a fist and ready to strike. I began walking differently and my outer appearance began to change. I developed an "I don't care" attitude about everything. My parents probably saw my change more than anyone else.

Though I lived in a two-parent home at the time, my dad was seldom around. He worked a lot, so our mom was the primary disciplinarian. The problem was, she often went overboard with the discipline tactics. Unfortunately, for me, I was the oldest girl which meant I took the brunt of all of her beatings. I know my mom loved us, but her disciplinary style was horrible. Most likely, she did to us what had been done to her in her past. I couldn't do anything about or say anything to anyone about the beatings.

One day, I asked my aunt to talk to my mom about the way I was being treated by her. Her response to me, "what happens in your house, stays in your house." That was the moment when I knew, I truly had no one. I felt alienated and hopeless.

When I was eighteen years old, I joined the Navy to get away from life as I had known it, but as you know, it doesn't matter where you may go, life will always follow you. I began looking for love in all the places and trying to fill the emptiness I felt inside. I even had a one-night stand with a guy I barely knew. As a result, at twenty, I became a mother to a son, and I knew nothing about how to raise a child. I gave my child everything I had, which left me depleted. Again, I turned to pornography, only to find that it left me feeling emptier inside. I spent lots of money to support my habit; Pay Per View Channel, "skin a max," better known as Cinemax. I never bought pornographic magazines into my home because I never wanted my son to find them.

I even sought happiness on the internet. Being online lead me down a path I said I would never go. My online search led me to a person whom I thought I would live the rest of my life with. I met a woman and entered into a lifestyle of homosexuality. When I met this woman, our friendship became the best I had ever experienced at that point in my life. We remained friends for about two years and eventually became a committed couple. We had a solid relationship, and I didn't need to indulge in porn anymore because she filled all of my voids. I was happy and enjoying life. I proposed to my girlfriend, gave her a ring and promised to be with her forever. I had only three years left in the military. Once I was finished, I had plans to move to Canada. I was sure that I had found my soulmate, and then, God interrupted my plan!

God was trying to teach me something: Walk out of it the same way you walked in it with your eyes wide open. In other words, you knew it was wrong when you walked in it, now it's time to walk out. I ignored the signs for about three months, but God kept knocking at the door of my heart.

In March of 2006. I finally surrendered and said "yes" to God. I gave Him my "yes," at a time when I was still deeply in love with my partner. I was in a tug of war for my heart! I was in love with both God and my partner, but not committed to either one of them. I told God, "I can't live without her. He said, "You can't breathe without me."

After four years in a great relationship, I ended it in obedience to God. Afterwards, I felt like I was dying. Literally. I didn't know it, but I was dying, dying to my sinful nature and to my flesh. When God called me, He began to transform me. All I did was agree with him. I kept saying, "yes" to him. It did not matter how I felt, how much I cried or if I wanted to give up, I kept giving God my "yes!"

I surrendered my heart to Him every second and every minute of every day. It was just me and Jesus, no counselors, just Jesus and His Word! I discovered that it wasn't about religion, but about a relationship with Jesus. The bible says in *James 4: 7-8, "Therefore submit to God. Resist the devil and he will flee from you. Draw near to God and He will draw near to you. Cleanse your hands, you sinners; and purify your hearts, you double-minded."* It says in *1 Corinthians 6, "to flee or run from sexual immorality."* Again, *James 5:16* tells me *"to confess my sins one to one that I can be healed."* We all need a community of support; we can't do it all by ourselves, we need each other to be healed.

I'm grateful to God for the journey of freedom. Someone, or even you, may be stuck and thinking you are the only one going through what you are dealing with right now. Today, I share my testimony to help you and many others become free. Someone is waiting to hear our stories.

Jesus: The Power of Testimonies

I wonder how many times I have been asked to share my testimony. I would recant the story of my life, give a few scriptures, and end with "You Can Make It!" One day as I was driving to work, I felt a conviction resting on my heart. Although a testimony is simply a story of what a person has been through, there is something that I can never leave out, and that is Jesus! I can never leave out the importance of my Savior. I almost felt the need to rewrite my story to make sure people understand that although my life wasn't a bed of roses, and I was a child who suffered much brokenness which spilled over into my adult life, Jesus has always been my sustainer. There are so many people who are mentally "jacked up" from molestation and rape. There are people today who are dead and, in their graves, because they could not handle the pressures of life. As I look back at all of these things, I know it could have been me.

I remember being suicidal and feeling full of emptiness. I remember trying to understand love, yet never grasping its concept. I could never understand or feel love from my family. I knew they cared about me, facts; I knew they loved me, but I did not know how to receive it. The doorway to my heart was nailed shut and I was unable to receive anything. The reminder I received while driving in my car was that Jesus was the only one who I couldn't receive true love from. Jesus in His grace and mercy, came and pulled out the nails that had closed the door to my heart and He lifted and opened the door. He alone began to fill the voids within my heart. There was nothing no one could have ever done to fix the broken pieces of my life. There were no words of correction that could have been said to undo the hurtful words spoken over and to me. There is no eraser that could erase the memories that are stored in the filing cabinets of my mind. Only Jesus is big enough to handle such a task. If I am honest with you, initially, I didn't even think Jesus could take the pain away. I mean, doesn't the bible say, *"he will never leave you nor will he forsake you?"* This statement here had to be one of the most troubling things I could hear. It made me feel like Jesus really didn't care about me, or I was a joke that He created. I am just keeping it real with you.

There were tons of pain I carried as a young girl. I must say that God created the female person to be strong. God put within every woman the ability to be a modern-day superhero. We can see this when we look at *Proverbs 31*. The sad thing is, so many women feel as if they can never measure up to a woman of such virtue; I beg to differ. If we were to step back and think about all that a woman does and has to endure, we have to wonder, where does she get the strength and tenacity to do all that she does? Well, the answer is women were birthed with that capability. Isn't that something to think about? It is because of this capability; I could experience so much as a young person and still be able to smile.

Please don't get it twisted, the smile didn't mean I was doing okay. My smile represented the tears of a mighty inner rainfall. No one understood my pain. I honestly felt like no cared. So here I am, a child being raped by five fifth grader, and the only thing I can remember is having to explain why I was so late coming home from school. The next memory is of me going to each of the boys' houses and made to tell their parents what happened and then to my school officials to share the same story over and over again. The boys were suspended, and I received some candy. Yes, candy. What child wouldn't love to get candy? The problem with getting the candy is that it was not good therapy for a child who had been through a traumatic experience. This was the trend in my life. I wasn't always given candy, but wearing a smile became the mask of my pain. I was overlooked and I felt like no one ever really cared about me.

Now don't get me wrong, I had a family that appeared to be fantastic from the outside. I was so proud to say that I had grown up in a two-parent home. I can remember waking up on Saturday morning to my dad making breakfast for us. I also remember our fishing trips, and dad made sure we had money for Sunday school. After we found a church home, Dad woke up early to get us to church on time. I have many wonderful memories of family trips, going fishing, camping and picnics at Keystone State Park. Unfortunately, some of them were overshadowed by a dark cloud that no one could see. I was a girl with the "upside-down frown." I must have worn it well. If I think back in time, I can see myself smiling, never once crying. On the contrary, if I looked closer, I can see a little girl who was soaking wet and drenched in tears of her own pain.

Bully & Fear: My Childhood Enemies

Have you ever been bullied? This is for the person who, like me, had to literally run home from school every day. Sometimes, I wish I could go back in time. I would ask each person what was it that made them want to fight a person, particularly me. There was no casual walk home for me when I was in elementary school. I had to run home or try to get out of the school before everyone else did. Why? My guess is that I was the "quiet" girl. I was the student with a smile on my face and I was different in a lot of ways. The sad thing is, no one knows what a child is going through or why may they act like a "goodie two shoes." That is what I was called by my peers. None of them knew what my home life was like. They also did not know that if I had gotten into a fight, it would have led to harsh punishment for me at home. So, I continued to smile. I showed no emotion because the callousness of my heart had begun to form.

Fear is something I understood well. Fear isn't necessarily a bad thing. In my opinion, when fear is a respect of consequences that guides a person to make good decisions, it is a good thing, however when that fear is derived from people who are bringing you harm either verbal or physical it usually is wrong. Often times, it results in a person being controlled by dictation that leads to a form of abuse. That is my personal definition of fear, and I am sure it is one that many people can identify and relate to. My definition of fear is what transcended from my school classroom all the way to the place I called home.

Every home has its comforts; everyday wasn't a bad day, but I didn't have a lot of good days. If you had seen me, you would have thought I was one of the happiest children you ever had known. I walked around with a smile planted on face, but my smile equated to tears. At home, smiling was the wall I built to keep people from asking me questions. My smile was my protection, but at times it caused me so much trouble.

I can remember standing in front of both of my parents as they were correcting me for something, I had done wrong. My response to them was with a smile and not with tears. My parents said, "Take that smile off your face," or "Kim, if you don't wipe that smile off your face, I'm going to slap it off." Unfortunately, for me it didn't matter what was said, the smile usually stayed and the slaps and beatings followed. The callousness of my heart continued to grow thicker.

My home life was diverse. There were moments of great laughter and fun, yet there was also a dark overcast that followed me no matter where I was. So those moments of joy often ended up with me feeling totally abandoned. It had become easy to share the bullet points of my testimony, the accounts of what happened to me, but rarely do I talk about how I felt while growing up. Children are very resilient as they take a beating and keep on ticking. There must be a survival mode button that kicks in when the abuse starts, because I am not sure how I survived. But I did. Let me pause for a second and give God some praise. You see, as an adult, I found myself wondering why? Why didn't anybody do anything or even say anything? Why? And every answer feels like a gut blow and a right hook to my head. In other words, all that I ran into was a lack of care. As an adult, I went back and spoke to several youth leaders that I had as a teenager for answers. For the most part, everyone said the same thing. In their own words, "I knew something was wrong." You knew something was wrong and you did nothing? Let me tell you as an adult, that hurts.

When I was a young Kim, I just thought my youth pastor was more interested in the guys. Most of the boys in our youth group didn't have fathers at home. He tried his best to be a good male role model, but his attention was more towards the ones who struggled in school for one reason or another. In other words, if you were not causing problems, you probably got overlooked. What was odd to me, was I clearly remember my sister getting a counselor. My brother had a counselor but why didn't I? I wanted to talk to someone too. I was overlooked. I wore that smile, and to everyone, that meant Kim was okay. But I really wasn't. I hated life with a passion. Dying seemed much better than living; I tried cutting my wrist. I studied and found out that in order to be successful, the cut had to be a certain way. I grabbed a razor blood, but baby let me tell you, that was some pain I wasn't willing to go through. Nope not that self-inflicted pain. I have a scar on my wrist to this day from that. I decided that if I was going to die, it had to be a way that would not cause me that kind of pain. I have taken pills, and I drank a mixture of products that should have torn my stomach up, but it didn't. I did it right in front of my siblings while they cheered me on. When they told our parents, I denied it all. I mean since I didn't get sick from it, why admit it? I was mad that it didn't work. I was mad that no matter how many pills I took, I didn't get sick. I was looking for a way to be noticed, heard, and seen, even if the meant laying my dead body in a casket. People would be sure would see me then. Obviously, my plan didn't work.

I concluded that I had to muddle through life. God cared about me too much to let me die. My brother and sister couldn't stand me because I was my mother's angel. I was the one that rarely got into trouble because remember, I was "Miss Goodie Two Shoes," and that carried over from school to home life. Being completely honest and transparent, I had terrible memories of beatings. Terrible memories of that and even as an adult, sometimes those memories still grip my heart. It is God that is healing those places. However, as a child, survival mode is real. The beatings were so terrible that we were left with bleeding welts and bruises. It didn't matter what happened. Sometimes you didn't know what happened. You only knew you better duck, run, and hide. But somehow, I made it through. It's funny as children once the beating is over, you just moved on until the next time. Ironically, I didn't even know how bad the beatings were because in my mind as a child, that was a regular occurrence. If we did something wrong, a beating was expected or at least some sort of punishment followed. "Spare the rod, spoil the child," was all we heard. There was a time when I could recognize that the beatings came when someone else did something wrong. Somehow, there became an unspoken responsibility put on me that I could not fulfil. The older I grew, the worse it got. I didn't know what to do. Every day wasn't bad, but there wasn't a day that I didn't walk in fear. You know children are resilient. It's like they have a mind that says, "I forgive you", "I love you", "It was my fault", "I shouldn't have done that", "I'll be nicer". But once we begin to mature and our eyes are open to the perpetual pain, something happens on the inside. An anger began to rise within me, a confusion happened that left me wondering, "Does anybody love me?" It will make one ask questions like, "Can you see the real me?" "Does anyone really care?" These were all my feelings.

The Conclusion of This Matter: Parents Matter

I mentioned that my mom called me her angel, but that was a distorted sound. I hated it. My dad called me by name, and I wanted to be just like him. I wanted to work on cars just like him. I wanted to fix things around the house. I wanted to be in control of something because everything around me felt like it was drastically falling apart. Maybe if I learned how to change brakes, it would get him to see me, but it wasn't me that he wanted to teach; it was my brother. Yes, my dad would allow me to hand him a tool, but I never learned any of that car maintenance stuff. I guess it just wasn't something a girl should do. In my mind, I thought I could do anything a boy could do. At that moment, my interest began to shift to electronics. If it was broke, I tried to fix it. I went from electronics to carpentry. My dad was always excited to hear about the projects I was working on and that made me feel good because I wanted my dad's approval. I longed for it. My dad was pretty supportive, but then he showed me where that line stopped.

Our dad was pretty much a man of his word; which was good. But the one promise that was made without words was, "I will be there for you no matter what." That was not the case. When our dad left home, it felt like my protection left too. When he left, it also opened the door to an adverse relationship with him. My parent's separation and eventually divorce was a cutting blow to my heart. My dad made sure we knew that although he was divorcing our mom, he was not divorcing us. But to a child, to me, it felt like it. The empty words of "You act just like your mother", felt like the sharpest darts being thrown at my heart. The pain of an absent father is unfathomable.

I can remember my dad trying to show us that he loved us. I have vivid memories of certain things like Valentine's Day. He bought my sister and I individual heart shaped cakes and gave us both a rose. My dad thought the jester was nice, but it only caused more frustration in my heart. The pain of hurtful words spoken from my dad caused a major wedge between us. As I got older and the callousness of my heart grew thicker, I chose not to speak to him for a few years. Eventually the silence would break because I missed my him so much, so I called him on the phone. That began a brand-new beginning for me.

I enjoyed the idea of having my dad back in my life, but something seemed to be missing. Even as an adult, especially my first few years in the military, the one thing I knew for certain was my dad was proud of me, but I felt like I was nothing more than a trophy to him. In my head, I was happy to settle for at least that. But was I really? That was the question. I had to come to grips with my own feelings of hurt and emptiness. Though I had specific memories of my mom that had left scars, at least I could say she never left. She was there when I needed someone to keep my son. She came to visit us. My mom became someone I could call upon if needed, and she never said no. However, with my dad, I never even considered asking him for anything. In my mind, I always thought his answer would be "no." That all changed in January of 2003.

I had to travel to Denver, and I needed someone to come stay with my son. As mentioned, my go to person was my mom, but this time I had this strong urge to ask my dad. I asked him to come watch my son, and when I tell you, the "yes" from my dad made my heart leap for joy. This was the beginning of a new start with my dad. When I picked Dad up from the greyhound bus station, he began to apologize for all the stuff he did and didn't do from my childhood to that present day. I couldn't even believe it! He said, "I'm sorry for the things I didn't give much thought to as an adult, like you playing tennis." I was a good tennis player as a child and got better as I got l older. The more it interested me, the less my parents supported me even down to buying shoes. He said, "I'm sorry," and he acknowledged that he missed the mark in certain areas. Do you know what that did to my heart? It became like and eraser to the bad, and a start line to the future. I knew at that moment I had my daddy back.

My mom has never apologized. I don't know that she ever will, but I do know that my mom loves me. She never left us. She made sure we had food to eat. She has been a constant support and I am so thankful for that. Truth be told, I am grateful to max for my mom. I would not have made it twenty years in the military if it wasn't for her. As I finish up this segment of writing, it is noticeable that the segments of writing on my dad is short while there was much more about my mom. That was in direct response to the length of time spent with each person. There is more about my mom because she was there, and I don't take that lightly at all she was. I love my parents so much. It has taken a lot of work on my part to not see them through my brokenness. Today, I see through much clearer lenses when it comes to life.

Though my pain ran deep my parents never had the ability to bring healing. Yes, the conversations helped, and the apology did too, but what I really needed neither of my parents could provide. I needed to know that Jesus could heal my pain, that he could take the broken pieces of my heart and mend them. It took most of my life, to realize that. It wasn't until December of 2010, that I finally grasped the fact that I had it all wrong.

My life began to take a turn for the better in January 2011. I met someone who turned out to be a good mentor. I stopped hiding in church and
began to allow my Pastors to help me. I thank God for my Pastors because
there was a level of freedom that I received just by opening my life to
them. I never thought I would trust them the way that I do. That is a
testament of God grace and mercy over their lives and mine.

It is my prayer that somehow my story has or will help you to "unmask." If you ever need someone to talk to, this is my invitation to reach
out. Feel free to email me at Kim@bridgesofhope.community.

May God give you the grace and mercy to lay down all that you carry
and unmask.

Kimberly Johnson, is a native of Pittsburgh Pennsylvania, where she resided until the age of eighteen. Kim proudly served in the United States Navy for twenty years and honorably retired in 2009. Upon retiring Kim attended Saint Leo University where she received a Bachelor's degree in Religion.

Over the past seven years the Lord provided her an opportunity to mentor hundreds of women dealing with same sex attraction throughout the United States, as well as various countries.

Kim currently is an active member of Bridge Church in Virginia Beach, Virginia where she serves in the Children's Ministry. She is the founder of Bridges of Hope Community; a group that fosters healing and hope for the hurting.

It's Not About Me

Healing from "It's Not About Me" by Cynthia Rose

I dedicate this chapter to every child, whether boy or girl, teen, adult man or woman. If you are reading this, it is possible that you may have or may be experiencing some form of abuse. My prayer is that as you read my story, it will give you hope and will bring you into the knowledge that freedom for you is very close -- just reach out for it!

My hope is that my story will inspire, encourage, and motivate you to seek out the help that you need to begin unmasking your pain and healing your past. Furthermore, I pray that it will reflect some commonalities to ensure you that you are not alone in your situation. You are loved, and you are capable of loving. Your God given gifts and treasures are waiting to break free! *"For I know the plans and thoughts that I have for you, says the Lord, 'plans for peace and well-being and not for disaster, to give you a future and a hope (Jeremiah 29:11 AMP).*

Isn't it interesting how God gives each of us the power of choice? On the contrary, there is an area in our lives where we do not get to choose; we cannot choose our parents nor our family members.

It is true that bad things happen to innocent children who also do not have the power to choose. Children are physically unable to protect themselves when they are subjected to abuse and perverse behaviors at the hands of an adult. Whether the abuse is by molestation, sodomy, rape, mental, verbal, physical, or emotional abuse, as the young victim gets older, they will tend to blame themselves.

As a result of abuse, children will develop distorted views of what is considered to be right and wrong. As they grow older, the way that they view love or truth, what is considered to be authentic, their own identity, how to trust others, how to control their anger, all of it becomes tainted when one has been abused. In fact, the anger can become so intense, that it can be difficult to see; blinding even. Yet, a child will continue to search for love, but often in all the wrong places and in the wrong people.

Why did God let this happen to me? Why am I here? Many victims of abuse never find the answers to their "why" because they likely resort to suicide, rather than choose to live. As for me, killing myself was never an option, at times, I just didn't want to exist or BE! Thankfully, God had a plan for me and my future… I simply could not see it.

Here is my story…

In 2006, during a sleepless night, I wrote this journal entry:

"Sometimes I find it hard to sleep, so I write. When I am asked to talk about myself, I get stuck, because there are so many things about me. In order to make sense of it all, I would have to talk about my past which was filled with trauma and drama. Sometimes, I am reluctant to talk too much about me too soon, (it's my stuff, but I'm still working on it), nevertheless, I would like to tell you more about me, but I need to start from the beginning or at least, my beginning."

Train up a child in the way he should go [teaching him to seek God's wisdom and will for his abilities and talents], Even when he is old, he will not depart from it. Proverbs 22:6 (AMP)

The bible says, *"children are gifts from God,"* (Psalm 127:3), and His Word instructs parents on how our children are to be trained; yet, they themselves have not been trained properly. Some parents have been troubled and abused, and our issues, along with personal life choices is what shapes the foundation of who we are and what we become, not who God has created us to be.

For You formed my inward parts; You covered me in my mother's womb; I will praise You, for I am Fearfully and Wonderfully made; Marvelous are Your Works, and that my soul knows very well. Psalm 139: 13-14 (NKJV)

A Functionally Dysfunctional Foundation

God formed and covered me in my mother's womb. He knows me, my entire life, the good, the bad and the ugly. "I AM" created me, therefore, my past does not define me. God created me especially for this day and this appointed time, to encourage you! YOU ARE FEARFULLY and WONDERFULLY MADE!

I was born and raised during the Holiness Pentecostal Movement, in a fire and brimstone, "scare the hell out of you" church. Seriously.

I am the eldest of six children, and as I write this, it has suddenly dawned on me, that my Mom married my father when she was just fifteen years old. It was her first marriage.

My mother was born in Augusta, Georgia. She is the youngest of her siblings. At the age of nine, she moved to Washington, D.C., to live with my grandmother. While there, she attended District of Columbia public schools and met my father when she was in the tenth grade. Exactly how they met is still a mystery to me. They were married and had a total of five children.

I was born on February 17, 1959, two weeks before my mother's sixteenth birthday. I was wise as a child. Although, I tried my best to be obedient, on the inside, I lived in a quiet rage for many years. When my anger button was pushed, I would just "flip out." Growing up, I had many other challenges. Sex was one of them, because I equated sex with love. My siblings also had and still have their own challenges. I mention this because the exposure to abuse, physical or otherwise, has affected all of us.

In that same year, ten months after my birth, my sister was born on December 31st. She has one daughter. My sister's challenges were with drug and alcohol addictions. Two years later, in 1961, another sister was born. I don't know which month she was born in because she later died from Sudden Infant Death Syndrome (SIDS).

My first brother was born on January 3rd. He has been challenged with repeated incarceration and drug addiction. He has four children. Lastly, in 1963, my second brother was born on August 16th. He has a daughter and a son. He has followed in our brother's footsteps of going in and out of prison. He was convicted of allegedly committing homicide and is currently serving a life sentence.

Growing up, I can remember my Mom having to work an average of two to three jobs, which kept her from home most of the time. Although, she was very young when she had her children, she worked long and hard to take care of each of us. We had all of our basic necessities and when possible, we could get some of the other things we wanted.

She always encouraged us to get a good education, attend Sunday school and church services, and to participate in various ministry departments. As a young married woman, I am sure she had her own challenges. Especially being married to a husband who drank alcohol and had no desire to go to work, nor was he capable of keeping a job.

My father physically abused my mom and did not care if he did it in front of us. His abuse left us all physically, mentally and emotionally scarred. My mom remained strong while having to endure her own pain while striving to be the best mother she could be to us. She was a disciplinarian, and her expectations were high, especially for me, because I'm the "oldest." I had to be the example for my younger siblings and was made to be responsible for chores and household tasks that they didn't want to do. If the chores were not done, I would get into trouble. My siblings and I called mom "crazy" when she was upset. Ironically, it is the same thing my own children have said about me.

When we misbehaved, my siblings and I got our butts whipped and we were "popped in the mouth" on the spot, wherever we were. There was no waiting until we got home. Then, there were times when we were restricted from going outside which was the worst for a child. I had many arguments and fights with my sister and brothers because their chores weren't done which meant I had to do so much more before Mom came home.

Trying to raise five children with an abusive husband, while living in a dysfunctional environment, is a recipe for catastrophe! Mom finally was able to escape with the help of my grandmother and her best friends, mom's godmother and godfather. At the time, I was about three or four years old.

My biological father was not in our lives after my mother escaped from him. He had never been much of a father to us, and frankly, I did not feel the loss, nor did I have any desire to know him as I grew older. He had always been mean-spirited and abusive. How could I lose what I never had? My father had never made an effort to get to know any of his children. We had not gone missing, nor did we move out of state, and he knew exactly where we were. At a young age, I clearly understood that he did not want to know us and that is what I concluded.

My father died sometime in April of 1987, due to complications associated with alcoholism. I do remember that his funeral was around this time because I had suffered a miscarriage during my fifth month of pregnancy.

My sister called me and said, "everybody is waiting on you!" Everybody was actually my mom who was concerned about what people would think about her during this time. I didn't understand why she wanted me to attend the funeral of the man whom I never knew and who did not desire to know me. I can only assume that she wanted me there because I am the "oldest" of their children. At any rate, I was not interested in going to his funeral. Reluctantly, I went, but only because mom wanted me to.

Prior to his death, I had gone to see my father in the hospital. I didn't want to go there either; again, I went because she asked me to. What do you say to a father whom you never knew? I had nothing to say, there was no emotional connection or attachment to him at all.

At the funeral home, I did not go up to view my father's body. My sister had asked me if I wanted to see him, and I replied, "for what?" I just went to the back of the room and sat down. I cannot tell you what happened from that point on, even if my life depended on it. I can only remember shutting down my emotions, raising my walls of defense and blocking out everything that happened that day. Afterwards, I went home.

I asked myself, "how could my father be a good father to us based on the example my grandfather had set for him? Could it be that my grandfather too, was a hellraiser, alcoholic, and abuser? My grandfather also died of alcoholism. I don't remember ever having one conversation with him. I remember that he was usually quiet until he started drinking. To this day, I have no idea when he died, nor did I attend his funeral.

Mom married a second time to my stepfather and my third youngest brother was born in 1966. My brother died from complications of HIV/AIDS and is survived by one son. It was said that my stepfather died of cancer, but I am inclined to believe it was something different.

I helped my mother with my stepfather's funeral arrangements, along with the arrangements for my brother, grandmother, and uncle. As a matter of fact, in helping Mom with my stepfather's funeral arrangements, I began putting my creative writing talents to use. I assembled and printed the funeral program for his Homegoing Service and later became known as the go to person for creating wonderful memories for other family and friends. Wow! In writing this, I just discovered another hidden gift.

The Abuse

The Lord is my light and my salvation—Whom shall I fear? The Lord is the refuge and fortress of my life—Whom shall I dread? When the wicked came against me to eat up my flesh, my adversaries and my enemies, they stumbled and fell. Psalm 27:1-2 Amplified Bible (AMP)

At the age of five, I started attending school. Every day, my grandmother would walk me to and from school. In our apartment building, was a family with a teenage boy who lived underneath us in the downstairs apartment. While my grandmother and mother worked, soon they trusted the boy to walk me from school and take me home until I was picked up by one of them. It was convenient since we lived in the same building.

One day, the boy picked me up and took me home. I sat on the sofa waiting for my grandma to come get me. Out of nowhere, the boy decided that he would try and make me lie down. I immediately jumped up. Next, he tried to remove my panties. I panicked and held tightly to my panties so that he could not pull them down. I kicked and screamed for him to stop! I was literally scared out of mind because I did not understand what was happening to me. There was one thing that I knew for sure, I had to keep my panties on. I put up a fierce fight for a five-year-old. I used all the little strength I had to keep him from getting my panties down. It worked.

When he heard my grandmother coming, he tried to shush me. He said, "you better not say anything." He made me sit up like nothing had happened; I was crying and still scared. I don't remember if I told grandma what had happened, but I do remember that he never took me to school again. It's hard to believe I was nearly raped that day! I knew that God was real at a young age. He gave me the strength to fight against my attacker, although I was no match for him. God dealt with the abuser in His time and in His way.

My siblings and I had a nine o'clock bedtime, the only exception was if we were out at a function. One night, I was awakened by my stepfather. He told me that my mother wanted me to come downstairs to her room. I followed him and asked no questions. When I got to their room, my mom was not there. I asked, "Where is my Mom?" He lied and said she would be back soon. I told him I wanted to go back to my room. He said he wanted to play a game first, and I said, "okay."

He made me get into their bed, and he began asking me questions about boys. Then, at some point, he tried to pull off my panties and began touching my private parts. I frantically tried to get away from him, but he pinned me down. I was no match for him, and I was terrified!

He began touching me and rubbing me with his penis. He asked me how did it feel while he also made me touch him. He said he would kill my mother, my sister and brothers when I said I was going to tell my mom. He told me that if I did tell her, she would never believe me. He continued to threaten me as I continued to cry and yell for help. At the same time, he told me that he loved me the most. It was sickening. When he was done ejaculating, he sent me back to my room. My mother never showed up to save me. I was only seven years old.

My abuse by my stepfather spanned a period of eight years. It happened at times when he was drunk and sometimes when he was not. I could never tell when the attacks would happen or when I would be awakened from my sleep.

My stepfather was careful not to sexually penetrate me. I am not sure why he didn't rape me, but it changed nothing of how these bouts of abuse had affected me emotional and mentally. He made me feel dirty.

I began taking lots baths or showers. When I put on clean clothing, I still felt helpless and unloved. I finally wrote a letter to my Mom to try and explain what was happening to me, but I never gave it to her. I found the letter three years later when we were moving, but I tore it up. At the time, everyone seemed happy and I didn't want to be the one to destroy our family.

I was fifteen years old when he made his final attempt to molest me. This particular day, I had PMS (Premenstrual Syndrome) and my hormones were raging! He came into my room. I was in bed and had been drifting in and out of sleep. I was feeling miserable from the very heavy and painful menstrual period. He knelt down beside my bed, and smelled like a barrel of old liquor. I could feel his presence beside me, but I did not move. I opened my eyes and said, "If you don't get the hell away from me and out of my room, I will kill you! If you ever come in here again, I promise that you will not live to see another day." I never moved a muscle until he had left my room. When I knew he had gone, I bolted up and swung the door open. I could see my sister coming up the stairs. I know that she must have seen our stepfather leave our room. That evening, I told my mom what happened.

When I told my mom, she said, "I do not know who to believe." I was crushed, and it only confirmed what my stepfather had said. My mother stayed two weeks in my grandmother's room before going back to sleep with her husband. Of course, her denial did not help me or the situation. I only became angrier because I could find no support at home. I don't know if grandma had an opinion about it or not because none of what happened was ever addressed again. We resumed life as usual...church, school, and chores. My only way out of this horrible ordeal was to get my education and graduate from high school.

Affect and Effects

As I write my story, I now understand that my abuse began with my biological father through alcoholism, physical, mental, and emotionally abusive behavior. I also recognize that the abuse continued at the hands of those whom Mom trusted and allowed into our lives. I do not blame her for what happened. I don't believe any parent wants their children to be abused unless they themselves are the abuser.

Another eye-opening truth for me was the "learned behavior" I had adapted to. As an adult, I chose similar types of men who were also abusive to me. They were wolves in sheep's clothing who were ready to wreak havoc in my life. I allowed them to control me, and they became physically, mentally, and emotionally abusive towards me. As a result, I was left feeling worthless and unworthy.

To cope with my pain, I developed a poor attitude. Depending on the environment, I could be respectful to some and act ugly towards others. I cussed like several dozens of sailors, but I was able to control my behavior in certain situations. In private, the cuss words flowed freely from me. In public, I was very watchful of people especially in new or unfamiliar environments. I did not allow many people to get close to me. If one had met me during this season in my life, they would ask, "Why is she so mean?" My physical demeanor spoke volumes, it screamed, "Stay the hell away from me! I don't trust any of you!"

I made a ton of mistakes and bad decisions while looking for love in all the wrong people. As a child, my virginity was stolen, and then, I gave it away at the age of thirteen. As a teen, I became very promiscuous. I was having sex for the sake of trying to feel close to someone. The feeling of being close never lasted long, and I always felt empty afterwards.

I started dating an eighteen-year-old. I skipped school to be with him. At the time, I was only fourteen, but my age did not matter to him. When I turned fifteen, I got pregnant. I didn't know it, but my 9th grade teacher sure did. One day after class had ended, Miss Ferguson, asked me to stop by her desk. When she and I were the only ones left in the room, she asked me, "When was your last period?" I told her, "I do not know." I really wasn't sure how many periods I had missed, but I felt I didn't have to answer her. Then she asked me again, this time, in a stern tone, "how many periods have you missed?" I said, "two."

She immediately marched me to the nurse's office and called my Mom to come to the school. Now, I was really afraid. My mother would have to leave work and come to the school and lose her pay. I stayed in the nurse's office until mom arrived. Miss Ferguson explained why she had asked her to come which is when I found out that I was pregnant.

My mom asked me several questions, and afterwards she went and spoke to the boy's mother. Together, they decided that I was not going to have the baby; Mom made me have an abortion. To make matters worse, I found out that my stepfather had bet my mother that I would be pregnant by the age of fifteen. What an awful seed he had planted in her head.

I nearly died having the abortion because all the placenta had not been removed, so the procedure had to be repeated. I was hospitalized for a few days, and I recovered at home and before returning to school. I was not angry with Miss Ferguson for telling my mom; however, I was angry at my mother and my stepfather. How dare he place a bet against my future! I blamed him for the most of the craziness that I had endured in my life. He was pure evil in my eyes!

It would be the first of many abortions I would have. I was pregnant a total of eleven times. To date, I have three live children, have had two miscarriages and six abortions. At times, I had beat myself up over and over about it. I believed I was going to hell according to the commandment, *"Thou shall not kill" (Exodus 20:13)*. I had done it six times!

I was lost, and I continued to live my life out of order and on my own terms. Sometimes, I went to church, then I stopped going. Most Sunday's, I attended "bedside radio or television church," since I could not find one that I wanted to attend. I was going through the motions. I had accepted Christ, accepted Christ again, and accepted Christ again and again. I re-dedicated my life to Him in a Baptist Church and then started studying with the Jehovah's Witnesses and non-denomination groups. I was a hot mess! I was all dressed up on the outside, but I did not believe that God would ever forgive me for the wrong I had done. I was with men who were either married, single, or in a relationship. It did not matter to me. What good was I to God?

My first serious relationship was with my first husband. He is the father of my two older children. We connected some months after my first abortion. I was able to talk to him about many things, including my abuse.

We dated all through junior and senior high school and moved in together during our senior year. I was eighteen.

His uncle helped us by co-signing the lease and we were soon able to get a one-bedroom apartment. I had to leave home. I wanted to kill my stepfather. Life was not great, and my stepfather and I could not get along together. He always spoke negatively about me to my Mom, and she became strict with me, but not with my other siblings. They seemed to get away with everything!

When I wanted to go somewhere, it was like being in an interrogation. They wanted to know who, what, where, when, how long, what time, and get phone numbers. At the time, I thought it to be so unfair. I later realized, in her own way, my mother was trying to protect me from making unnecessary mistakes while wanting me to complete my education.

Life with the boyfriend was different, and not at all what I expected. We had some great times, and we also argued and broke up many times. He even left me, but then he came back.

At nineteen, I became pregnant again. Life after our daughter became more difficult. I was in college and he did not want to "babysit" his own daughter. Eventually, I had to stop going to school because he would not keep her. If I wanted to go out anywhere, my daughter went with me. Her father was very controlling, and we would end up fighting, so I just opted to stay home. I sought counseling as I struggled to parent our child alone. It was depressing.

I went against the advice of others who told me to leave him. I was torn because he was the father of my child. We ended up moving to Maryland and had a son when I was twenty-two. We married the next year. I began to think, just maybe, I should have left him, but I was trying to keep our family together.

He began abusing me physically, verbally, and emotionally. I did not realize how much he had actively started using drugs until we separated. Of course, I knew about the marijuana. I smoked it on rare occasions. It made me feel weird, so I wasn't interested in drugs or alcohol, to be honest. I had seen all of the effects of substance abuse growing up. My addiction was to cigarettes. Thankfully, I was finally able to give up smoking in 2004. Today, by God's grace and mercy, I have been delivered from nicotine addiction for over fifteen years!

I started dating after my first marriage ended, which was not a good decision for me. I continued in that relationship for over a year, until I had finally had enough of it. I had abstained from sex and dating for the following year which I thought was a real accomplishment for me. I went back to being the same lonely and unhappy woman that I had once been. I was still very troubled and my mind was unsettled.

I went on my first and only blind date. I married a second time and gave birth to my youngest son when I was thirty-three. My blind date, who is also my son's father, was good with my two older children. He cared for them while I attended business school to pursue a career in Paralegal Studies. He helped them with homework, made sure they had dinner and a bath while I studied and researched legal cases. I became a certified paralegal, but I opted to become a legal secretary instead.

My soon-to-be husband, was employed as a Computer Aided Design Drafter. He accepted a job in New York City for more income. He came home most weekends, but some weekends he didn't come home at all. Then, there were the other women and the broken promises. His cocaine addiction was spiraling out of control. He signed up to start treatment programs but would never really attend the meetings. It was the most miserable year of my life.

Husband -to -be began doing the same crap he had been doing before. We had a joint checking account. I paid the bills and the checks would bounce. He started going on all night drug binges. I had seen this before, just in a different place and with a different abuser. The stress of the relationship eventually took a toll on me.

He decided to enter into another program. In this one, we both had to participate. I continued to attend our scheduled counseling sessions and meetings for co-dependent persons, Al-Anon, but he didn't come with me. I was finally done with him and was preparing to leave him. My only source of income at the time, was my children's child support check from my previous relationship.

One month the child support check did not come, so I called the Maryland Courts. They informed me that the check had been mailed. I knew Mr. Blind Date had taken it. I threatened to call the court to investigate if he did not return the check to me. He did, and I purchased several one-way tickets to Washington, D.C. for my children and I.

As time passed, he cleaned up and surprisingly, we did get married. Nonetheless, the same scenario started all over again. I finally asked him to leave because I was getting physically sick of being with him. Again, we attempted to reconcile but the drugs remained an issue. When we divorced, he did not even offer child support for his only biological son.

I could go on and on about all the negative things and people that have played a role in my life. To tell the truth, I played a major role in every event. I was the one who said, "yes," to the known and unknown messes that surrounded me. I allowed these situations and negative relationships to enter into my space. I had to break free! I had lost my peace, my joy, and my happiness at this point in my life. It wasn't until my baby boy and I went to counseling together that I was able to begin my road to real forgiveness and restoration.

Turnaround: Forgiveness Renewed My Mind

I love myself. I love my family. I have learned to trust. I am wiser. I am finally living my best life. No, I am not perfect, but I am nobody's victim either. I have chosen to leave my past, in the past. Now, it only serves as a reminder to me of where I was, and where God has planted me today. I know how to ask God for forgiveness for myself, and I forgive others quickly.

Matthew 6: 14-15, declares, *"For if you forgive men their trespasses, your heavenly Father will also forgive you. But if you do not forgive men their trespasses, neither will your Father forgive your trespasses. (NKJV)*

As a part of my continued therapy, I wrote a letter to my stepfather who is deceased at the time of this writing. It was important for me to express how I felt about what he did to me, and how I struggled for the entire month of July in 2006.

I don't know what it is like to have a real father in my life. I have never been a Daddy's girl, because I had no "Dad" in my life. But what I do know is my Heavenly Father, my Creator, the great I AM, spoke very clear to me, through my therapist and through the reading of His Word. If I do not FORGIVE others for their trespasses, no matter the hurt, pain and harm, then my Heavenly FATHER will not forgive me for the wrong, hurt, and pain that I have caused others, knowingly or unknowingly. It took me a while to get to this forgiveness thing, but I made it. I asked for help.

I have forgiven my stepfather for abusing me and taking my innocence away from me. I have forgiven my father for not being a father to me and my siblings. I have forgiven my Mom for not saving me from abuse. I have forgiven my husbands, as they really didn't know how to be husbands. I have forgiven all who have harmed, hurt and pained me in some form or another. Most importantly, I forgive me. I forgive ME, for believing that I was unworthy of love, happiness, and joy; for blaming others for my mistakes, my circumstances, my feelings, real or imagined, known and unknown.

I AM WORTHY and so are you! FORGIVENESS is freedom!

Philippians 4:13 asserts "I can do all things [which He has called me to do], through Him who strengthens and empowers me [to fulfill His purpose—I am self-sufficient in Christ's sufficiency; I am ready for anything and equal to anything through Him who infuses me with inner strength and confident peace.] Amplified Bible.

I know that happiness is within me, and I know that true happiness is in Christ Jesus. He has given me Peace, Joy and Love which surpasses all understanding. I didn't have to go looking for it because He was always there. I just had to let Him back in. God is not a man that He should lie, His Word is true! He will never leave nor forsake me!!

I cannot stress this point enough, "I am not my past and my past does not define who I am." I had some hard work to do which included working on me. I had to conscientiously change my thinking; what I believed, my behavior and who I was associated with. Because I know that I can do nothing in my own strength, it is by the Grace of God that I am where I am today, still growing in Christ Jesus! I am a Kingdom Dweller and God's plan for me has only just begun!

I am not a victim. I do not have a victim mentality, instead I chose to empower others by sharing my story to inspire, to motivate and to take action! It's not just about me!

Cynthia Rose, is a native Washingtonian. She was educated in the Washington, D.C. public school system and later attended The Washington Business and Technology Institute, where she received her Paralegal Studies Certification.

Cynthia is a servant of God and a helper to His Church Body. She is a member of Temple of Praise International Church, in Beltsville, Maryland. She loves people, music, art, and dancing. Among her many God-given gifts are event planning, decorating, sewing, crafting, painting, and writing among others; and she shares them all.

Cynthia resides in Hyattsville, Maryland. She has three children, three granddaughters and one grandson.

The Meal That Almost Killed Me

Healing from "The Meal that Almost Killed Me" by Crystal Rivera

We are Unmasking Nationally…

At a time like this, God revealed how relevant this story is to what is currently going on in the world. Right before my eyes I witnessed how God was unmasking the nation publicly. The plan was so strategic, that God used people of power to expose each other? Why was this happening and why now? Was God "sick and tired" of our immoral behavior that was being fueled by and increasing prosperity of those already wealthy? The reality was that anyone and everyone could be "unmasked."

Not only had I become unmasked, I wanted to be mask free! However, I must be honest, my journey wasn't full of willingness or honesty. I was like so many other people, DEFIANT! I had no idea that I would be stripped of everything right before my eyes because I didn't know the power of surrender.

One Sunday afternoon, I decided to watch "Super Soul Sunday" on the OWN Network. Oprah interviewed Representative Beto O'Rourke; a Democrat from Texas. I heard Oprah ask Rep. O Rourke about the idea or thoughts of running for President of the United States. It is in that moment; I became teary-eyed and full of emotions. Why? Not because I would vote for him, but because I felt HOPEFUL for the world. This is the same HOPE I felt when I began to unmask for the very first time. I want you to know that HOPE is a place that I want to live time after time. However,

HOPE has neighbors like Faith, Surrender and Courage who are waiting for us to knock on their doors.

If you are thinking of "unmasking," remember, it is never too late. *Deuteronomy 31:6* states, *"Be strong and of good courage, do not fear nor be afraid of them; for the LORD your God, He is the One who goes with you. He will not leave you nor forsake you".*

I need you to know that writing this story has been one of the hardest things I have ever done. Why? For two reasons; some parts of this story have triggered me emotionally, taking me back to several places of pain. Secondly, I am writing it in a way that you can connect to this story without me exposing the book I am currently writing.

"At the age of 40, I went to jail for 1.5 days and had to sleep on my mother's sofa for 2 years because I smoked crack cocaine from 1987 to 1999. In 2014, I was convicted in a way that I had never been before…" This is reference to my current project.

There will be stories, testimonies and books, but nobody can tell my story better than me. Why? It is embedded in my heart and soul for the rest of my life.

One day I will not be around to tell this story, but people all around the world will be able to read what I have written. It is written by me because I lived it, I felt it, I breathe it, I inhaled it and exhaled it!

"God doesn't Microwave, He Crockpots" - Pastor Dan

"The Meal that Almost Killed Me," is a metaphorical memoir of a 3 Course Meal. I want to take you on a journey in a way that would not allow you to read about another person's life that had a traumatic childhood and ended with a great testimony.

I want my heart to reach your heart through compassion, empathy, and love. I'm hoping spirits would become awakened thru self-identification. Ultimately the spirit of God's love would be an everlasting drink.

I believe the international love language is food. People all over the world fellowship over food and drinks daily. I have written the comparison parts of my life to a very simple meal. Each course has its own special ingredients and flavorings. I have thought carefully about each course that has been the most influential in my life. Do not be hoodwinked by the simplicity of the meal. This is a meal of great supremacy affecting the brain. Anything that affects my brain affects my behavior. My behavior needed supervision most of my life.

I recently attended a CPR class thru my employer. I was informed that when a person dies from a heart attack it is because of the lack of oxygen to the brain. Could it be that the way I was living was giving me moments of decreased oxygen to my brain? Absolutely! The good news is that I am fully aware of it today.

In this memoir, I want to expose some of the most toxic ingredients that have truly shaped and formed me into the person that I am today. Nevertheless, forgetting about those things that were liabilities and assets at the same time. If I looked through different lenses, they would and could change my whole life at different times. Does that sound complicated to you? It really isn't! I'll reveal that in the next story.

God revealed to me two things as I was writing this story:

- I had parental seasonings that still had an aftertaste long after the meal.
- Was I able to survive from drink alone?

Please sit down and get comfortable as we break bread together. I hope you enjoy the meal!

MENU:

Appetizer: Fantasy Fruit
Entrée: Transformation Soup
Dessert: Rock Candy Cookies
Beverage: Everlasting Water

*Remember that God has the right to change this menu at any time. Some items may be out of season or discontinued. Depending on what season you are in, ingredients could be diverse.

There are no substitutions for **Grace** Corn and **Mercy** Carrots, however you may substitute Pain and Misery for Surrender. Di-cy Potatoes are available once yearly due to the cost.

Please let God know if you are paying with his blood or yours. Don't forget to please leave a tip for yourself.

Therefore, I urge you, brothers and sisters, in view of God's mercy, to offer your bodies as a living sacrifice, holy and pleasing to God—this is your true and proper worship. Romans 12:1 NIV (New International Version)

Fantasy Fruit

I was first introduced to fantasy as a young child through television during my most influential, formidable years. The popular television show "Leave It to Beaver" caught my attention and took me out of my world and into what appeared to be the closest thing to perfection. I was attracted to their lifestyle, language, and problem-solving. I was attracted to it because I didn't understand why my dad couldn't be like Ward Cleaver? Why couldn't my mother communicate to her family like June Cleaver? Why didn't our house look like theirs? Why, at the end of the day, did everyone go to bed happy, no matter what?

As I grew up, I had to be reminded that this was only a television show with people who were acting. This was not real! What was real was happening in my own home. My childhood was not perfect. My parents were not perfect, and neither was I. I was focused on my family liabilities for many years because of fantasy. It wasn't until I began to "peel the onion" and go deeper through writing that my family assets were revealed. I then became grateful for everything I had endured.

Marriage was also a fantasy I had to get out of my parent's house. On December 10, 1983, I married my first husband, only to go back to my parent's house after the honeymoon. I was 25 years old. What was so wrong with me that I couldn't have what other people had?

The fantasy fruit I ate was mature and connected to some of the ingredients in the rest of the meal. The fruit began to take me to dark places emotionally. This lead me down a path of an isolated, dishonorable, yet creative passion. However, even though the afterthoughts would leave me feeling shameful, I would continue to eat the fruit. Eventually, the fruit lost some of its power and my longing for it decreased. I later found out that the only way to stop eating the fruit was to change some of the ingredients in the soup? How could this meal be so toxic, relatable, and have an indescribable taste that would follow me the rest of my life?

"I AM" Soup

As a young adult, I was pretty much forced to learn how to cook. My mother just stopped cooking one day, and I had to figure out what I was going to eat. I was a teenager at that time, and I knew how to cook several dishes. I decided that I was going to teach myself how to cook from one of the 20 "Southern Cooking" cookbooks my mother had around the house. Of course, it took many practices, as I remember the garbage can being available for me. So "If you first don't succeed, try, try again" was really meant for me during my cooking journey. I can say today, that I am a "cook extraordinaire," which means, "I can throw down!"

My father's mother, "Grandma Lizzie" was the best cook I knew. I'm not surprised they paid her to work in the school cafeteria in Newport News, Virginia. Grandma Lizzie is the only person I know that could make chicken and dumplings from scratch the way she did. I can remember that my father was a great cook as well. I could always tell what he was cooking as the smell drifted all the way from the kitchen, down the hall and into my bedroom. My favorite was fried chicken smothered in home-made gravy. Nobody could make gravy like my daddy, except his mother. That's probably how he learned to cook as well.

My father used to make a chicken vegetable soup that caught my attention too. I really thought it was the most amazing thing I had ever eaten. I can remember the freshly diced white potatoes and the split chicken wings. I can still see my father spooning up the hot vegetable soup as he smacked his lips with happiness. The juicy chicken wings couldn't fit on the spoon, so you had to dip two fingers into your bowl of goodness and capture your wing that would be demolished in five seconds. Today, I often create my soup with chicken wings or wingettes, just like my dad did. I had no idea that the journey of family meals had left such great memories. I hope this triggers your own memories of good times of family and food.

My life has been like a pot of soup that serves as the main course. My journey has been influenced by each ingredient and flavor. The SOUP story has been simmering for a very long time. I want to inform you of the dictionary definition of simmering. It means "keep (food) just below boiling when cooking or heating it." Thank God my story commenced below boiling. I often thought the longer the pot of soup simmers the better it would taste. However, the more you eat, it appears that this pot of soup never runs out. My SOUP has often had an interrupted simmer. I think sometimes it appeared it was simmering on top, but the bottom was cold. Also, sometimes, folks would judge the soup based on its appearance and suggest that it wasn't good enough and should be discarded. However, God sees the good in everything because *Isaiah 46:10 (NASB) says "Declaring the end from the beginning, and from ancient times things which have not been done, Saying, 'My purpose will be established, And I will accomplish all My good pleasure".*

This pot of soup used would be small when it first started cooking. The ingredients were tender, innocent, and fresh. Some ingredients were placed there before I could talk; **Grace** Corn, **Mercy** Carrots, **Prayer** Peas and of course BOJ sauce. The pot of soup was always transforming. Internally and externally the sauce seemed to always transfer from one pot to the next. Sometimes, I would add ingredients to the soup and later discover their toxicity; **trauma** noodles; **self-hatred** rice; **denial** garlic; **low self-esteem** tomatoes to name a few would end up in the soup. At first, I didn't know if I added courageous chicken or not. I knew I would need to add surrender shallots, green beans of deliverance, and ultimately di-cy potatoes. I needed all these ingredients in order for my life to change.

Because I was born with sin, God knew I would need Grace and Mercy. As the pot began to simmer, I began to look for love in all the wrong places and I tried to fit in everywhere I went. I had an identity crisis that was connected to several ingredients.

The trauma noodles were first connected to the warzone I faced some days as I grew up. The trauma was suppressed and I was never asked how I felt about anything. My father had a drinking problem and my mother had a problem with it. Today I know my father's way of coping was thru alcohol, but where was his pain coming from? I believe he was only doing only what he knew how to do at the time. There was generational alcohol use in my family and the noodles were no stranger to this soup. These noodles had been there a long time before I was born, and they were tired. There was a noodle with my name on it waiting for me. Even though I was a late bloomer, I eventually picked up alcohol too. At some point I started sneaking some in my dessert. I remember that first bite of those **Rock** candy cookies like it was yesterday. Because I had diverted from the soup, something on the inside begin to happen to me each time. I didn't like where I was in my life and Self-hatred rice rose to the top of the soup. Every time I didn't want to face what was really going on, I could add denial garlic. What do you do when you are in denial about being in denial?

I was twenty-nine years old when I realized my mother noticed something different about me. The pot of soup had been neglected. Why hadn't my mother noticed it before? I had always wanted my mother to tell the soup how much she loved it. The soup was lonely and felt stagnate. In 1987, when I started eating those rock candy cookies, that is when an adversary sold me some rainbow homo beans to add to my soup. The color of the beans made me very enthusiastic and inquisitive. I wasn't given much information about the formation of the beans, but I was informed I would be surprised as I added them to my soup. The taste of the delightful colored beans took me to a place of intense euphoria and external metamorphism.

Initially, the beans made me excited about how my life was changing. I was influenced to eat the beans in the beginning, and then I just volunteered to eat them for the next twenty-seven years. I began to believe in who I was becoming, and I made you believe this was who I was. The beans changed everything about me. I internalized the spirit of the beans and began to mimic complete obliteration of my life. My mother watched me as I continued to morph into a person that she didn't know. I begin to indulge in sexual immorality the more I ate the beans. I want to believe because of this, my mother began to increase her prayer life like never before. My mother was confused, disappointed, and probably thought she had failed me as a mother. But did she forget I saw her sleep many nights with her Bible beside her? Those white pages reflected a light of hope. I know that same light was somewhere, in the bottom of that soup even though I could not see it. My mother did not know that she could protect the soup from the homo beans if she had just covered the top of the pot with her loving arms while she inhaled every defected ingredient as she exhaled her vulnerabilities. If my mother would just stir the soup. It sounds like a simple thing to do, but some days, just picking up the spoon felt so abnormal. Was it because her mother didn't stir her soup?

Must the world give another label to the pot as having a "generational curse?" God, are saying that I can no longer blame my family for the way this soup turned out? At this point I had to start taking responsibility of how I wanted my soup to enhance the lives of others that were struggling just like me. I began to look for different ingredients and began to scoop those things out that were contaminating the soup.

Rock Candy Cookies

In 1987, a co-worker asked me if I had ever had rock candy cookies. I had no idea what he was talking about, but I became immediately interested in this fine dessert. I was shown how to make the cookies and all the ingredients I would need. Initially, I only ate the rock candy cookies on weekends, but I had become a slave to the taste of them and my greatest fear was running out. I became addicted to the **Rock** candy cookies for twelve years. I connected with other people who were addicted to them and hung out with them in the "shadiest" places. I couldn't figure out how something so small had so much power over me. These cookies always kept me longer than I wanted to stay and had me spending more money than I ever had. I even thought if I started selling cookies, I would never run out, but I became the cookie monster! It was illegal to sell rock candy cookies, but the euphoria made me feel empowered, and I became a local representative. A monkey can't sell bananas and a cookie monster can't sell cookies! Could it be that the fantasy fruit appetizer had influenced my thinking even the more? Or, was it the low self-esteem tomatoes in the soup that reminded me I wasn't "good enough?" What?? I'm the "local representative" with a beeper and a flip phone!

Most children are taught to eat their meal before they eat their dessert. Of course, I didn't do that because I couldn't get the taste out of my head from the first bite. I begin to become obsessed with these rock candy cookies. Eventually, I'm eating more cookies than soup and I begin to transform physically, mentally and spiritually. I didn't even notice the progression of the addiction to the cookies and how my life had become unmanageable. I had several episodes in 1998 with the law enforcement involving these rock candy cookies which eventually lead me to a brief detainment in Newport News City Jail. You would think I would stop this erratic behavior after experiencing such a traumatic event. I was released from jail and immediately returned to the lifestyle with rock candy cookies. I realized that I was facing serious consequences with the court system and I needed a power greater than me to help me get through this ordeal. Well, I found that "power" that was greater than me on sentencing day. You'll have to wait for my autobiography to be released to get those details.

However, I can say in 1999, I lost the desire for those cookies and the lifestyle. I stop eating the rock candy cookies and found a new way to live. Several years later, I noticed that my life was very much still unmanageable. I eventually acknowledged the power of those toxic ingredients as they manifested in all areas of my life. You are probably wondering "how could this be?"

Let me explain with an example: The relationship I had developed with the rock candy cookies lead to obsession and compulsion. Once I tasted the cookies, I couldn't stop thinking about them and eventually I had to go get some. The process of obtaining the cookies became risky business each time, because I was willing to do whatever it took to get them. This cycle happened repeatedly for years. However, after surrendering and no longer eating the cookies, obsession and compulsion did not go away. I noticed that I began to obsess and act compulsive over other things; shoes, clothes, and cars to name a few. This type of behavior created financial unmanageability and total chaos in my life.

The Meal Changes

Over a period of years, the spirit of the soup would change because the ingredients were altering. My spirit awakens as I acknowledge the Grace and Mercy each time the soup is attacked by rivals. The trauma noodles and the self-hatred rice of the soup would decrease. "Common folks" began to notice that there is something extraordinaire about the soup. The soup begins to feel "loved" just the way it is. In 2013, God showed me an ingredient that would change my life profoundly. Spiritual Di-cy potatoes. These potatoes reminded me over a course of five years of how much God loved me. However, I sat with the impression of conviction of my foolishness. God gave me the courage to continue to eat through my fear because the green beans of deliverance would be poured into the pot just like oil. There would be a fresh anointing over the soup that would amaze those who witnessed it. Why? Because the darkness leaves and the light in the soup has been reignited.

Remember the BOJ sauce in the soup earlier? I had discredited the one thing that kept the soup from drying up and dying. It was the BOJ sauce; the most important ingredient in the soup because it was the foundation that had supernatural powers, deliverance, and forgiveness of my sins. It was the Blood of Jesus that was preparing me for everything in life. It was my personal weapon that could protect me. The BOJ sauce reminded me that fantasy fruit was a trick. It removed the obsession and compulsion of rock candy cookies and dried up every colored homo bean in the soup! How can this be? There had to be an intensification in the temperature, which would cause the sauce to boil, strategically killing off those things revealed. God revealed that this fiery transformation and regeneration wasn't enough to seal the deal. There would be more commitments and assignments delivered to sustain a life worth living.

You are free when you realize you belong no place- you belong every place- no place at all. The price is high. The reward is great. – Dr. Maya Angelou

How to live without Salt and Pepper

We know that every good recipe needs flavor. The one thing that most people use consistently in their recipes is salt and pepper. My salt and pepper were a team even though they were very different. They didn't look or act alike. On most days they had better outcomes if only they worked together.

My mother's caregiver died August 27, 2003. He had taken care of my mother as she battled diabetes as an amputee. He washed my mother, helped to put her clothes on, cooked for her, and took her to her doctor's appointments. He was a retired postal worker who still wore his modified uniform to do yard work. He loved to go and sit on a stool and pull the weeds out of the garden around my mother's azalea bushes. Those azalea bushes bloomed every year and most of them were pink. Those azalea bushes were special because they added vibrant beauty to the front of the family house.

If you would look at my mother and her caregiver, they would appear to be a perfect match. There was something special between them. There was a different kind of love that you would never understand. Her caregiver was her husband for over 50 years. He was my father.

My father knew his time was short on earth as he disclosed his diagnosis to his family. We had a family meeting one evening as he laid his insurance papers and funeral arrangements down on the table. My father says, "I'm ready to go, and there is no need to spend lots of money on a funeral". At the time, we knew it was real and dad had accepted his cancer diagnosis. Dad eventually was placed on hospice at home. He now needed his own caregiver as his wife was in the other room, needing someone else.

My father and I had a good relationship. I remember as a child at a very young age, I would wrap my legs around his ankle as I sat on his shoe as he carried me. I felt like I was on a ride as he walked through the house. The other greatest memory was when I got my first bike. It was a "banana bike" with high handlebars. I was so excited one day as my Father called for to me outside to get on it. I rode it in the middle of the apartment complex around on the square shaped sidewalk, going around and round. There were training wheels as it leaned to one-side. I beg my father to take the training wheels off at this time as the I am feeling courageous on this day. I watched as dad carefully took the wheels off because he believed in me more than I did. I got up on that seat of a bike as he held me steady. I had both hands on the handlebars and both feet on the pedals. As I began to ride as my father let go, I was off into the wind. Then all of a sudden, there was a crash! I learned a great lesson that day. The lesson was that sometimes you have to take a risk in order to go to the next level. And in taking that risk sometimes the outcome can have consequences. The other thing I learned was that when you fall, there might be a little pain, but all you have to do is get up and try all over again. I had a bloody knee!

In September of 2005, we memorialized my mother eighteen months after my father passed. I remember the day like it was yesterday. The most beautiful thing I remember was the peace I saw on my mother's face after so many years of health challenges.

See, my father was my salt and mother were my pepper. My soup could never be made without salt and pepper! We are consistently adding these core flavors to our meal. Each dash is influential to me. They are the flavors that I needed throughout my entire.

However, the day your salt and pepper are gone, you still remember the taste just like it's still there. How does this happen? Because the spiritual taste has been absorbed into every ingredient. Salt and pepper had been around for a long time and enhanced my life tremendously. Today, I realized the shakers are empty, mom and dad are gone, but the Soup survives. When your pot is made by God, good stock will be absorbed into every surface, "nook and cranny". The salt and pepper shaker may be empty, but the spirit of the flavor will continue to remind you of who you are.

Sometime in your life when you eat a meal that almost kill you, your antidote might be **Everlasting Water**. Are you courageous enough to drink water and sacrifice the meal set before you? Why is it that water has the most important function in everything we do, but we deny the power that water has? Did you that water comes in 3 different forms, gas as a water vapor; solid as snow and liquid as rain? It is only the power of God that could create something so undeniably magnificent. Water represents life and Christians are Baptized with or in water.

Water baptism is a beautiful picture of what our Lord has done for us. As we are completely immersed in the water, we symbolize burial with our Lord; we are baptized into His death on the cross and are no longer slaves to self or sin (Romans 6:3–7). When we are raised out of the water, we are symbolically resurrected—raised to new life in Christ to be with Him forever, born into the family of our loving God (Romans 8:16). Water baptism also illustrates the spiritual cleansing we experience when we are saved; just as water cleanses the flesh, so the Holy Spirit cleanses our hearts when we trust Christ. (https://www.gotquestions.org/water-baptism.html)
This is the best meal you could eat and it's everlasting…

Meal Planning Guide (Self-Care)
1. Do not let your plate become a "platter".
   - Do you feel like you just can't say "NO" sometimes when you are asked to attend an event?
   - Are you staying late at work and nobody asked you to stay?
   - Did you plan a vacation recently or went on vacation and worked most of the time?

2. **Use fresh fruit**
   - Invest in yourself; "You are what you eat"; Pray often for discernment as you make choices in every decision you make; Stop waiting for the "free food"; Growth will cost you something.

3. **Always look at the expiration date.**
   - Those things that are unhealthy could be contagious; The whole family/team can be affected; Last year's ingredients could be toxic to your purpose. Some relationships need to end;

4. **If it doesn't taste good doesn't always mean it isn't good.**
   - Change is hard, but continuous; Growth doesn't feel good and requires us to step out of our comfort zone; Sometimes we must eat what we don't like because it is necessary.

Continue the Journey Until We Meet Again…

Tell Yourself: I found out I was different and different was good! I spent most of my life trying to be someone else because I didn't know I was good enough to be me. Why? Because you didn't tell me…Then I found out I had the power to tell myself.

As I continue my journey, I have learned many things about myself. Each journey has begun with surrender and courage. I must embrace my pain and relieve my own suffering. I must not allow false pride to get in the way and I must ask for help publicly or silently. I must listen to those who know more than me.

I have learned to stay humble by helping others less fortunate than me. I have developed a passion to serve and care for those in need. I believe in "quality of life" for all. I have shifted the power from people to Jesus. I'm learning to "just be with Jesus" and stay in the moment. Why? There is light in all darkness, if I would just stop waiting for it and just acknowledge it! I will find peace in the storm no matter how big it looks.

Every day, I'm learning how to love better, speak wisdom, dream and work toward my purpose. What does your journey look like? Peace and Blessings!

Crystal Hayes Rivera is a Hampton, Virginia native and graduate of Hampton University School of Education. Crystal had to make a professional career change in 1999, when she became attracted to the "street life" and could no longer teach. Crystal began to believe God had her on a journey that was going from darkness to light. The career change eighteen years ago, empowered Crystal to serve individuals that were just like her.

Rivera is currently working on her first book, "The Sofa," which will be relatable to many as one learns to surrender over and over again. Crystal currently resides in Virginia Beach, Virginia, and works in the city helping the underserved and homeless population.

Self-Rejection: The Band-Aid That Didn't Stop the Bleeding

Healing from "Self-Rejection: The Band-Aid That Didn't Stop the Bleeding" by Simene' Walden

As Amazon begins to remove its stories of healing, deliverance, and identity issues as it relates to homosexuality, I knew that my story was imperative for such a time as this. While I do not believe that God is only concerned with our sexual desires, proclivities, or preferences, I do believe He was unwavering when He commanded us to be fruitful and to multiply. You can't exactly multiply God's way when you are living contrary to what He has ordained to be; marriage with one woman and one man.

My story stems back to when I was a young girl in middle school when the seed of rejection was planted deeply in my heart by my own father. I can remember it as if it were yesterday; he called me to inform me that he was driving to Florida with his wife and two other children to spend a week at Disney World. Why would he call me to say that? What was going on in his mind that he would call me to share good news and not invite me? I never understood why a father would do that to his first-born daughter.

As the years passed by, I had the opportunity to talk to my father's first-born son who had shared my exact experience. Our father had also called him about his trip to Disney World. For the life of me, I have no idea what would make our father call us to say that. He probably called us on the same day (but I'm not sure). Maybe one day I will get a chance to ask him.

For the first time in my life, I felt a sense of sadness and grief that I could not articulate nor knew the words to say to express it. I just knew I was sad and I cried for days. My mom was so upset with my father for making me cry that she called him back and laid him out. I never told her exactly what he said, but she knew I was sad and I was crying. Whatever he had said to me, she was going to let him know that it was not "okay."

All week long, I thought about the fun my dad was having with his new family. Question after question ran through my mind and I wondered for years, why was I not good enough? Why wouldn't my father spend money on me for things that I wanted and experiences I desired to have? I wondered, why did he go to court and lie about his household income so he could continue to send eleven cent child support checks to my mom for years? When the tables turned for a bit, it was a whopping $111.00 per month, but in my head, that was not enough because he could take a week off to spend in Florida with his wife and two other children. I resented him and developed a deep seeded hatred towards him. I hated him and everything that was connected to him. I cut him off for years.

For almost twenty years, I wanted nothing to do with my father and I had nothing to do with him. I would talk to him occasionally, but nothing major. I did not want to be connected to any of his other children and for the most part, I didn't. I loved my aunts, uncles, and grandmother on my paternal side, but I also resented them because I resented my father for rejecting me. That same year started an emotional downfall for me.

I was sexually violated that same year by a man at least ten or fifteen years older than me, and I held that pain inside for years. I finally was able to share it with my mom January of 2016. Let me just put a mic drop here, because that was one hard conversation to have. She took the news well, or so I thought, but she later told me that her heart almost collapsed and she felt that she had not been a good mom. I had to immediately let her know that it was not her fault and she was the best mom for me. In those moments, I resented my father all over again. In my mind, had he not divorced her when I was two years old and left her as a single mom now to raise three children, she would not have had to work so much when I was a child. I was broken and I was bitter. I was mad at him. I had not forgiven him truly, even though I repeatedly told myself year after year I had. The truth was, I loved my dad and wanted him to accept him, but since he didn't that feeling of rejection and abandonment turned into pure hatred.

I became a very bitter little girl, and I grew up to be a very rejected, dejected, and wounded woman. I started to sense rejection from other boys, and I gave myself away sexually just to feel love. I loved my older brothers, and I wanted to be so much like them that I started to sneak and wear their clothes. They were about five times bigger than me, but I did not care. I wanted to be accepted and loved by them, so I did what I thought was right in my mind to connect with them. It all backfired.

Throughout high school, I became what most people call a "tomboy" and I loved to wear boy clothes. I just loved jeans and all kinds of sneakers. To this day, I still do. But in 11th grade, I attracted the attention of a classmate who started a rumor that I was gay and was liking her cousin. It made me mad, but I didn't really care because I liked boys and lots of them. The rumor persisted for a few months and then sizzled away. It was not until I was about to go off to college that my grandmother gave me the most bizarre and ignorant graduation "congratulations." Her exact words were, "Don't go off to college and turn gay!" Why in the world would an older lady say that to her granddaughter? Because in her mind, she probably thought I was already. Family can be a trip, but there is no perfect family, not even Jesus, so I will leave that alone and keep moving for now.

When I went to college, I met so many people but I met this girl who eventually became one of my best friends. Ironically, she was cool like me and dressed just like me. We just loved each other, laughed all the time, and didn't judge one another. I was still sleeping with boys, so I was cool with whatever people thought of us. I started attended "stripe bars" and gay clubs with her on a regular basis. I would watch the women and girls, but I was not interested enough to try anything with them. I couldn't bring myself to go "all the way." So, I just watched and listened to her stories. It was quite entertaining. The more I was in those environments, the more my curiosity was peaked. Long story short, I did finally do it, and I did it for almost seventeen years. Something that seemed so innocent, ensnared me for almost two decades.

The first lesson in this is watch the words that come out of your mouth, even if you think something about a person. Words have power and what my grandmother and one of my aunts had thought for many years had subsequently come out of their mouths.

Because I was broken and fatherless, I literally attracted women who were a mirror image of me. In each of my relationships, we always tried to mask our pain, but it came out through our relationship with each other. The first lesbian relationship was very abusive. It was only by the grace of God that I am not in jail for first-degree pre-meditated murder. It is only by the grace of God. I wanted her to die because she spoke so many word curses and negative things to me, over me, and about my family. I hated her. Intimate partner violence is one of the biggest problems that plague the gay community. It is not outsiders or church people who are attacking them, but they themselves are killing one another. Broken people attract broken people and continue the cycle until people are beyond repair. BUT WITH GOD, ALL THINGS ARE POSSIBLE.

For seven long years, I was in and out of that emotional, psychological, physical, mental, and verbally abusive relationship that was reciprocal from both of us. From my car being damaged, to her eyes being blackened, to my face being kicked repeatedly by her Timberland boots, to me trying to throw her out of a moving car on I-95, and me breaking the window in her mother's home to get to her, each level of violence between us persisted. It was horrible, and I did not know how to get out and I did not know who I could tell. So, I never spoke about it until the later part of the relationship when I was tired and ready to get out.

I can remember one night, crying out to God in my bedroom in Greensboro, North Carolina, to save me and help me leave her. He did help me, and I never looked back. I started attending church, attending bible study, but more importantly spending time with God and reading my bible. I didn't know much of what I was reading, but I kept reading and reading and reading. As a reading teacher, I figured the more I read, the more I would understand over time. And that has surely happened as I have used study aids, guides, resources, and my helper Holy Spirit to help me work through this text. For two years, I was free of any sexual activity or entertainment of women, but I allowed the enemy to come back into my life by way of an ex-boyfriend who was married and incarcerated. I asked God to deliver me from my ex-girlfriend but not from the lesbian life-style…at least not then. Perversion was heavy in me, so I still wanted to sleep with whoever I wanted to. I thought sleeping with a man was better than sleeping with a woman after fully knowing it was wrong since he was not my spouse either. The emotional relationship with my ex-boyfriend was short lived once again, and I soon became attracted to a young girl at my part-time job.

I was the stable one and she had parental issues. I was like a mom to her and it eventually became a very perverted relationship. She wanted to get out of her parent's house, and I was willing to take her in. We were together for almost two years when she had a sudden encounter with God at a retreat, told me it was over, and she never looked back. I was blown away. I was shocked, I was sad, I was mad, but I also wanted what she had.

I decided to draw closer to God even more, and I breathed in the Word of God daily. I was adamant about finding Him in my broken places, and I did. He healed me in many areas of my life. It was during that time when I was able to confess many things that had happened to me. I was able to confide in mentors and trusted women about the sexual assault, the abuse, and the rejection issues with my father and other males that had happened to me over the years. I was growing stronger, but I didn't allow the process to seal what God had started. I prematurely started privately sharing my story with people who would be used to ensnare me again.

This next intentional jump and fall was someone I admired because of her brilliance and beauty. Eventually, we became really close sharing about our past experiences realizing we had a lot in common. Because Simene' was still broken and looking for love and acceptance, I pushed myself on her and she eventually gave into me. Initially, I don't think she wanted to "go all the way," but she was quite flirtatious and "touchy-feely" with me. The second lesson in this is, if someone tells you that they struggle in a certain area, don't provoke them or put them in awkward situations by doing the things that you know or suspect will trigger them. Just don't do it.

This relationship was not as abusive as my first one, and by the second one, I was only emotionally and mentally abusing her. I felt better about myself because I never hit her. Do you see how twisted my mind had become? I felt bad about that for so many years because she eventually told me how painful and hurtful I had been to her. I apologized, but I don't believe she has truly forgiven me for the pain I caused her. When I last saw her, she was done with me. I have decided not to reach out to her again. It is what it is, and it is a done deal.

My last lesbian relationship was a turn of tales for me. Based on the perception we have of people because of their looks and outer appearance, we judge superficially not realizing the danger that lies ahead. We hurt one another, and we were mentally and verbally abusive to each other. It was terrible and it took God to heal my wound because I had fallen into a sunken place.

I relocated to College Park, Maryland in 2015, because of our separation. I hated every minute of it, but it has helped me to grow. There was no way I could have remained in Charlotte, North Carolina and remained sane. He had to move me away, and I could not travel back and forth there for a long time.

Two years after living in Maryland, out of nowhere, she contacts me through my Facebook business page. I had been sending her messages and emails for the last two years because she had blocked my phone number. She said she never received any of them. I am not sure if I believed it, but I was just happy to finally talk to her and share what had been on my heart. I thought she had been rejecting me, but when she said she never received my messages, something happened in my mind. It was all I needed to hear in order to be back into the arms of the woman who suggested I move to Maryland, and also the one who had dropped me when I found out she had been back with her ex a few months before I moved. To be devastated was an understatement. I was crushed, but I had gotten a little stronger over the last two years and I wanted to see what would come out of our friendship this time.

I met up with her one Mother's Day in Maryland, and it was really good to finally see her after those two plus years after having no contact at all. The love and desire for her was immediately rekindled in my heart. Why?

Because it never left. I was taking a class in Upper Marlboro, Maryland called, "All Things New: A Discipleship for Unwanted Same Sex Attraction," for eighteen months, but there was a part of me that still wanted to see if I could be better for her after I got some additional help and support. Do you see how twisted our minds can be at times? I was getting discipled about more healing in my areas of brokenness, and I wanted to take my healed places back to something that was broken and could never work. We tried for about three months and it ended with disaster and calamity. Because I never closed that door completely, the enemy crept in a year later and I found myself falling all over again with another girl I met through a coaching program for about two months. Talk about disappointment, condemnation, and pure shame.

I have had to really work through my issues to get to the root of the problem. The only way I am still standing is because God keeps holding me up. Bloody, bruised, and beat down, God has held me up. With the help of a pastor who prays for me and teaches me how to pray for myself, my accountability partners, the therapy session I participated in, the continued counsel from my spiritual mother, plus my desire to surrender all, I have progressed at a rapid rate.

The third lesson in all of this is no matter how many times you fall, get back up. Believe in what God believes for you and listen to those He sends your way to walk with you through your mess. Discipleship, mentoring, and accountability can be messy. You must be honest about where you are so you can get the help you need in those areas. I was emotionally in bondage to this woman who was the epitome of what I thought a woman should be for years. This year, I was set free emotionally when I began to see myself as the woman I had always wanted to be with. I realized that it was "me" who I had been searching for since 8th grade. The rejected little girl was looking for wholeness and acceptance. When the scales and deception came off my heart, I realized this last relationship was leading me to hell, and I was the woman who would lead myself there too. Talk about a reality check. I had to really come to that realization that the spirits that attracted us to one another's final destination was hell. Despite how much I wanted to be with her and how much I desired her in my mind, we were not good for one another.

The fourth lesson here is watch out for cycles and lapses in time and then make sure you guard those entrances to your heart by blocking all access when it shows up. It is not "if" it will show up, but "when" it shows up. In addition to that, at some point in our lives, we have to decide between what God says and what we will do. I had to decide I will do what God says regardless of how I feel until those feelings align with His plans and Word for my life. I encourage you to do the same. Be honest about where you are, find wise counsel, and do the work. I applaud you for reading this book as this is the next step you will need to "unmask" so you too can heal. I pulled off the band-aid of my suppressed pain of rejection so I could stop bleeding. Jesus already bled enough on the cross. He receives us, and He will align us with those who will also receive us with no hidden agendas and dirty motives. It is time to now live and live abundantly in our souls and in our savings account. Say, "pain, pay me!" For every struggle, disappointment, and pain you have ever experienced, it's time for your pain to pay you restitution. Tell your story. Open your mouth and tell your story. I will be waiting to hear how you too, have *unmasked to heal*.

A native of North Carolina, Simene' Walden grew up in Northampton County, North Carolina where she attended Northampton County Public Schools. During the initial five years after graduating high school, she pursued her education at three different colleges only to find herself back where she started: Fayetteville State University. In 2004, Simené graduated with a Bachelor of Arts degree in English & Literature from Fayetteville State University. Ten years later, she obtained her Masters of Arts degree in Christian Studies with an emphasis on Youth Ministry from Grand Canyon University.

Simene' is a teacher, coach, writer, International Speaker and Trainer and an Amazon Best Selling Author. She believes in being teachable and remains in a posture of learning even from those one may not think has anything to offer. Simene' believes that everyone has something to offer. Simené's primary objective is to empower, educate, and equip others as she teaches them everything she has learned.

She is the Chief Operating Officer of *The Student Teacher,* where she is flooding the Educational System with God's Words of prayer and practical principles for daily living. The Student Teacher helps overwhelmed, overworked, and burnout teachers reignite their passion for this now and next generation by teaching them how to have the heart of a teacher and not just the content and knowledge of one. The Student Teacher LLC helps new and novice authors craft their stories without losing their voice and compromising their faith. Simene' is the author of seven self-published books and co-author of two book anthologies. She has done multiple book tours and hosted several events. The Student Teacher LLC will release the first self-published anthology with some amazing ladies early fall. Simene' is also a Travel Agent who not only meets your travel needs, but excels them.

.

Contact the author:

simene@simenewalden.com

http://www.simenewalden.com

https://www.facebook.com/simenewalden

http://www.twitter.com/@simenewalden

http://periscope.tv/@simenewalden

http://instagram.com/simenewalden

https://www.linkedin.com/in/simenewalden/

Additional Books by Simene' Walden

- Standing on His Words: Prayers and Devotionals Every Educator Can Pray, Published April 2017
- Standing on His Words: Prayers and Devotionals Every Educator Can Pray Action Guide, Published January 2018
- Spiritual Combat, Published August 2017
- My Heart Under A Microscope, Published September 2017
- Co-Author of Prayer Quake, Published October 2017
- The Student Teacher Quotes, Published November 2017
- Free Yourself, Published February 2018
- Co-Author of NC Girls Living in a Maryland World,
- Published August 2018
- Mathematics of God, Published September 2018

All books can be ordered from www.simenewalden.com.

Testimonials from "Standing on His Words: Prayers and Devotionals Every Educator Can Pray"

Both as an advocate for Moms in Prayer, an Educator and a mom myself, I find this resource to be invaluable! The power of prayer is monumental and we need it now more than ever! Excellent guide!
(Anita, Amazon Review)

As an educator, I recommend this book to my fellow educator as a reminder of why we do what we do. Get your copy today!
(Aikyna, Amazon Review)

This book is one to not only Read BUT keep out ON your desk!! Soooo many great insights and prayers for sooo many at different stages AND struggles as well!! GREAT reference!!! A Definite book to get for all!!!!!!
(Kelly, Amazon Review)

It is good you are sharing your gift with the world, and educators in particular. I haven't read a book on this topic yet. Thanks again.
(Deborah, Colleague)

I love this prayer guide. I read it daily. I'm a counselor, contracted by a large school district; Charlotte Mecklenburg Schools. I travel to many high schools and the powerful prayers travel with me. Praise God! There is power in prayer. Prayer changes things.
(Laurae Gilbert, Facebook Review)

Standing on His Words Courses and Seminars
Young Adults (17-24)

The Struggle Is Real: Parents Just Don't Understand

Do you often bump heads with your teenager and/or young adult? Do they feel like they are always being corrected for doing something wrong that they actually believe is right? Do they seem lost and frustrated because they want to create the life God has for them, but they have no idea what that is and what that looks like?

If you answered yes to either of these questions, this seminar is for your child!

This seminar will give your child real-solutions to very real problems in a very real and aggressive world. Within this workshop, teenagers and young adults will learn how to perfect the areas of concern in their lives from biblical truths and practical teaching.

The four modules will include the following:
1. How to create a blueprint for your life?
2. How to take the opinions of others and learn from them?
3. How to talk to God and get real-time answers?
4. How to focus on yourself and become the Best YOU?

Adults (25-40)
The Struggle Is Real: People Just Don't Understand

Do you often bump heads with people? Are you criticized about the way you see things and how you live your life? Do you often feel like the people around you do not relate to you and don't understand your viewpoint on many things?

This seminar will give you real-solutions to your very real problems in a very real and aggressive world. In this class, you will learn how to perfect the areas of concern in your life from biblical truths and practical teaching.

The four modules will include the following:

1. How to create a blueprint for your life?
2. How to take the opinions of others and learn from them?
3. How to talk to God and get real-time answers?
4. How to focus on yourself and become the Best YOU?

(Educators, Leaders, Administrators)
Creating a Culture of Collaboration and Respect

As the demands of excellence, production, and results are eminent, do you desire to respect all children regardless of their behaviors and interactions with you? Do you wish to respect and gain respect from fellow colleagues? Do you work in an atmosphere that could use some positive TLC?

In this class, you will learn how to create a place of peace in the environments that seem to be dominated by drama, negativity, and hostility.

The six modules will include the following:

1. How to create a culturally sensitive and affirmative environment?
2. How to create an Educational Environment not mirrored by the image of the Penal System?
3. How to protect yourself from being influenced by the accusations of others?
4. How to minimize distractions in the workforce?
5. How to honestly communicate with others even when angry?

Additional Seminars and Courses Include:

How to avoid "burn out"?

How to have the heart of a teacher and not just the knowledge of one?

Each seminar and course is a 4-hour session that includes the book and all other materials.

For booking inquiries and speaking engagements, please contact the author directly via email @simene@simenewalden.com

Testimonials from "Spiritual Combat"
This book gave me more scriptures to read for my healing and how to fight my enemies. This is a very good read.
(Victoria, Amazon Review)

This is a phenomenal read that will equip you for battle in the spirit realm. This book should be in every Christian soldier's arsenal!
(Brent & Angel Rhodes - Marriage of God, Amazon Review)

Spiritual Combat Workshop
Prayer Board

Does your life look like you envisioned it? Is your life aligning with what a parent, pastor, or prophet has told you? Has the Word failed you or have you failed the Word? Do you even know what the Word says about your situation and your life?

In this class, you will learn how to create the life you want by designing a visual prayer board of your necessities, needs, and desires from God. In this course, you will learn how to apply God's Words to your prayer request to obtain God driven and God given results.

The six modules will include the following:
1. Identifying your necessities, needs, and desires.
2. Finding scripture that answers your prayer request.
3. Gathering pictures that align with your prayer request.
4. Designing your prayer board.
5. How to incorporate the prayer board into your daily life?
6. What do I do once the prayer is answered?

Speaker Topics

(Inquire about other presentations and topics that has also been delivered).

- How to have the heart of a teacher?
- The Process Through Perversion
- Help! My Heart Needs Deliverance!
- Are We Free in Secret?
- Learning How to Prioritize
- Words Matter: Speak Life
- Dysfunction Between Mothers and Daughters (How to detect it and overcome it?)
- Do Not Be Ensnared by A Title (How to be free with titles?)
- Fruit Flies: What Happens When You Don't Use Your Gifts?
- From Frustration to Forgiveness
- How the Educational System Reflects the Penal System?
- Extreme Rejection for Divine Acceptance
- The Perfect Sin
- Religion and Relationships
- Same Issues Different Interest
- The Cost of The Anointing
- How Sick Are You? Some are physically sick while others are both physically and spiritually sick.
- I Will Finish Strong. (Drop-Out Prevention)
- My body is my temple. (Drug Awareness and Prevention)
- I Am R.E.A.D.Y. (High school graduates and college student's inspiration speech)
- I Made a B.A.D Decision. (How being **B**roken **A**lmost **D**aily lead me to the decisions I made and how I can turn my life around because of it?)

Simene' Walden's Signature Messages

- **Don't Lose ME** (Do Not Lose Your Morals and Ethics in the Marketplace)
- **The Heart of a Teacher** (What does it mean to have the heart of a teacher in your area of influence?)
- **The Speech That Quotes**

Resources Section

The resources that are listed below are tools that each other has personally used to find healing. To help with your "unmasking," I encourage you to consider some of these resources to help you on this journey.

https://bridgesofhope.community/
https://hiswonderfulworks.com/
http://www.loveatthecross.com/
https://uprootedheart.com/
https://desertstream.org/
www.bridgechurch.tv
https://thegatechurch.tv/
http://gotothetopic.com
www.deborabarr.com
www.pilgrimsministry.com
www.simenewalden.com

Artist Recommendations

- Tangie Callahan *It is Jesus*
- Tasha Cobbs Leonard Heart, *Passion, Pursuit*
- Tasha Cobbs *You Know My Name*
- Koryn Hawthorne *Unstoppable*
- Koryn Hawthorne *Speak the Name*
- Kurt Carr *One Church Project*
- Kurt Karr *Something Happens*
- Bethel Music *Raise a Hallelujah*
- Todd Dulaney *Your Great Name*
- Todd Dulaney *Victory Belong to Jesus*
- Tony Miller *Daybreak I & II*
- Jonathan Ferguson *Bootcamp Volumes 1-5*

- Dieko *The Psalms and Hymns*
- Brother Hahz *The Fixtape Volumes 1-3*
- We Will Worship *Like Oil*
- Derick Thomas *Unrehearsed Worship: Clean Hands Pure Hearts*

Music Recommendations
- Shekinah Glory Ministries
- Nathaniel Coe III
- Tiffany Anderson
- Shana Wilson

Author Recommendations
- Simene' Walden
- Rita Bowman
- Nike Wilheims
- John Eckhardt
- Kimberly Daniels
- Jonathan Ferguson
- Marilyn Hickey
- John Maxwell
- Ivory Hopkins
- Kenneth E. Hagin
- Debora Barr
- Sabrina Williams
- Patricia Miller
- Kathryn Kuhlman

Book Recommendations
- Holy Bible
- The Vines Complete Expository Dictionary

- James E. Phelan & Debora Barr *Practicing Exercise for Women Recovery of Same Sex Attraction*
- Rick Warren *What on earth am I here for?*
- Stormie Omartian *The Power of Praying*
- Stormie Omartian *Lead Me Holy Spirit*
- Michelle McCain Walters *The Esther Anointing*
- John Eckhart *Fasting for Breakthrough & Deliverance*
- Joel Osteen *The Power of "I Am"*
- Joel Osteen *It's Your Time*
- Cindy Trimm *The 40-Day Soul Fast*
- June Hunt *How To Handle Your Emotions*
- Nike Wilheims *Prayer Keys*
- Kimberly Daniels *Give It Back*
- Joy Lamb *The Sword of the Spirit The Word of God*
- Kristy Butler *Dating with Discernment: How To Avoid Courting with a Counterfeit*
- *The Gift of Discerning of Spirits* Kenneth E. Hagin
- *Words* Kenneth E. Hagin
- *Deliverance from Spirits of Sexual Abuse* Ivory Hopkins

Free Reading Apps
- Hoopla
- PDF Drive
- Overdrive
- Kindle
- Apple Books

Authors Recommendations

- Seek Professional Help. (Consulting with a believing therapist who share your moral and spiritual values as a Christian is highly recommended for those traumatic experiences. Trauma and deliverance are not the same.

- Talk to someone you trust (Accountability works if you are honest and do the work).

- Dance (Find you some upbeat, clean, and wholesome music to listen to).

- Go out alone. (You will be surprised at how much you learn about yourself when you are alone. Even if you cringe at thinking of going out alone now, you have to ask yourself why?).

- Paint (Any arts and craft store have the supplies you need but you can also participate in hosted paint parties around your city).

- Write (If you are in the beginning stages of sharing your story, start by writing it down whether through pen and paper or using an online tool. Whatever you do, get it out of you).

- Journal (Put your thoughts on paper).

- Learn something new. (In order to break old cycles and walk in the new, you will have to learn new things whether it is recreational, academically based, spiritually based, or professional based).

- Get out of your comfort zone. (Go to events and meet new people. Say hello first and show yourself friendly, so you can win a friend).

Other Recommendations

Reflections from Author Roberta Phillips

Reflections from Author Kim Johnson

Reflections from Author Crystal Rivera

Reflections from Author Cynthia Rose

Reflections from Author Simene' Walden

Message to Authors

Write a message to an author here, post it as a book review on Amazon, or post it to your social media and tag them, or simply send it to them.

Reflections from Unmasked to Heal

CPSIA information can be obtained
at www.ICGtesting.com
Printed in the USA
BVHW071428140819
555860BV00024B/1915/P